710

The ... f loan is normally three weeks.

The Voyage of Odysseus

The Voyage of Odysseus

Homer's Odyssey
retold by James Reeves

Blackie: Glasgow and London

© 1973 James Reeves

Illustrations © 1973 Blackie & Son Limited

ISBN 0 216 89630 4

Blackie & Son Limited
Bishopbriggs, Glasgow G64 2NZ
5 Fitzhardinge Street, London W1H 0DL

Filmset by Thomson Litho, East Kilbride
Printed in Great Britain by Robert MacLehose & Co. Ltd., Glasgow

Contents

Pronunciation Guide

This list includes the names of persons and places mentioned in the text. Roman equivalents of Greek names are in square brackets.

Achilles *(a-KILL-eez)*
Aeaea *(ee-EE-a)*
Aegyptus *(e-JIP-tus)*
Aeolus *(EE-o-lus)*
Agamemnon *(ag-a-MEM-non)*
Alcinous *(al-SIN-o-us)*
Amphinomus *(am-FIN-o-mus)*
Anticleia *(an-ti-CLAY-a)*
Antinous *(an-TIN-o-us)*
Antiphates *(an-TI-fa-teez)*
Antiphus *(AN-ti-fus)*
Aphrodite *(a-fro-DY-te)* [Venus]
Apollo *(a-POLL-o)*
Arete *(AR-e-te)*
Argos *(AR-gos)*
Artemis *(AR-tem-is)*
Athene *(a-THEE-ne)* [Minerva]
Atreus *(AY-tree-us)*
Calypso *(ka-LIP-so)*
Charybdis *(ka-RIB-dis)*
Cicones *(si-KON-eez)*
Cimmerians *(si-MEER-ee-ans)*
Circe *(SIR-se)*
Clytemnestra *(kly-tem-NES-tra)*
Corax *(CO-raks)*
Cyclopes *(sy-CLOE-pes)*
Cyclops *(sy-CLOPS)*

Epirus *(e-PEER-us)*
Eris *(AIR-is)*
Eupeithes *(yoo-PY-thees)*
Euryalus *(yoo-RI-al-us)*
Eurycleia *(yoo-ri-CLAY-a)*
Eurymachus *(yoo-REE-mak-us)*
Eumaeus *(yoo-MAY-us)*
Eurakus *(yoo-RAK-us)*
Eurylochus *(yoo-RIL-o-kus)*
Hades *(HAY-deez)*
Halitherses *(hal-i-THER-seez)*
Hecuba *(HEK-you-ba)*
Helios *(HEEL-i-os)* [Sol]
Hera *(HEER-a)* [Juno]
Heracles *(HER-a-kleez)*
 [Hercules]
Hermes *(HER-meez)* [Mercury]
Icarius *(i-KER-i-us)*
Idomeneus *(i-dom-in-AY-us)*
Ino *(EE-no)*
Irus *(EE-rus)*
Ismarus *(is-MA-rus)*
Ithaca *(ITH-a-ka)*
Jason *(JAY-sun)*
Laertes *(lay-ER-teez)*
Laestrygonians
 (les-tri-GOAN-e-ans)

Leda *(LEE-da)*
Leocritus *(lee-O-crit-us)*
Medon *(MEE-don)*
Melantha *(me-LAN-tha)*
Melanthius *(me-LAN-thee-us)*
Menelaus *(men-e-LAY-us)*
Mentes *(MEN-teez)*
Mentor *(MEN-ter)*
Myrmidons *(MIR-mid-ons)*
Nausicaa *(no-SIK-ee-a)*
Neaera *(NEE-e-ra)*
Neleus *(NEE-lee-us)*
Neoptolemus *(ne-op-tol-EE-mus)*
Nestor *(NES-ter)*
Oceanus *(o-SEE-an-us)*
Odysseus *(o-DIS-ee-us)* [Ulysses]
Ogygia *(o-JIJ-i-a)*
Olympus *(o-LIM-pus)*
Orestes *(o-RES-teez)*
Paris *(PAR-is)*
Patroclus *(pa-TROK-lus)*
Penelope *(pe-NEL-o-pe)*
Perimedes *(pe-RIM-ed-eez)*
Persephone *(per-SEF-o-ne)*
Phemius *(FEE-mi-us)*
Pherae *(FER-ee)*

Philoctetes *(fi-LOK-te-teez)*
Philotius *(fi-LO-ti-us)*
Phoenician *(fi-NEE-shen)*
Piraeus *(pi-RAY-us)*
Pisistratus *(py-SIS-trat-us)*
Polites *(po-LY-tes)*
Polyphemus *(pol-i-FEE-mus)*
Poseidon *(po-SY-don)* [Neptune]
Priam *(PRY-am)*
Proteus *(PRO-te-us)*
Pylos *(PY-los)*
Samos *(SA-mos)*
Scylla *(SIL-a)*
Sirens *(SY-rens)*
Sisyphus *(SIS-i-fus)*
Sparta *(SPAR-ta)*
Tantalus *(TAN-tal-us)*
Telemachus *(te-LEM-ak-us)*
Thebes *(THEEBS)*
Theoclymenus
  (thee-o-CLIM-en-us)
Theseus *(THEE-se-us)*
Thrinacia *(thrin-AY-ki-a)*
Tiresias *(ty-REE-see-as)*
Zeus *(zoose)* [Jove, Jupiter]

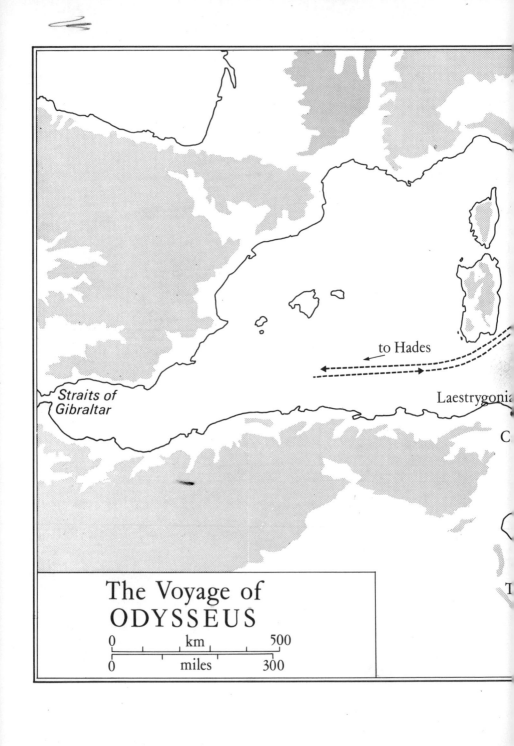

Straits of
Gibraltar

to Hades

Laestrygoni

C

The Voyage of
ODYSSEUS

0   km   500
0   miles   300

T

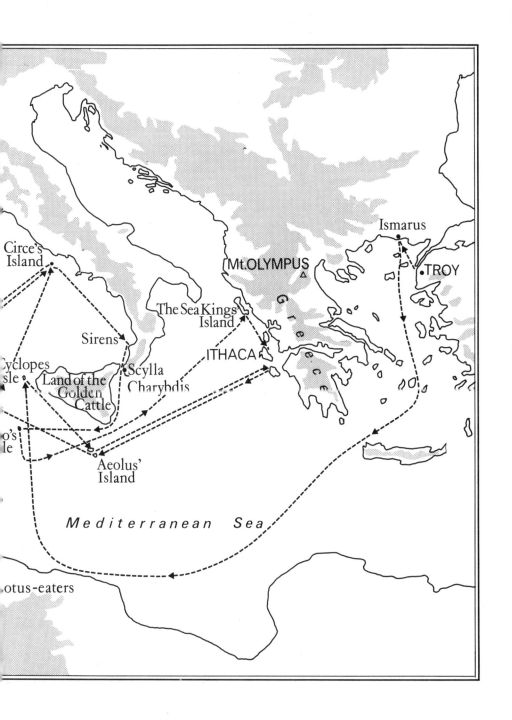

Circe's
Island

Cyclopes
Isle

o's
le

otus-eaters

Ismarus

•TROY

Mt.OLYMPUS

G
r
e
e
c
e

The Sea Kings'
Island

Sirens

ITHACA

Scylla
Charybdis

Land of the
Golden
Cattle

Aeolus'
Island

Mediterranean   Sea

PROLOGUE: THE TROJAN WAR

THE STORY OF Odysseus and his wanderings begins with the Trojan War, and the beginning of this war was a marriage feast. In ancient Greece everyone believed that the affairs of men and women were ordered and arranged by the gods, who lived in freedom on Mount Olympus. They were godlike because they could do as they wished, go hither and thither on the earth, interfering with the lives of mortals, from whom they expected continual prayer and sacrifice. But they were also like men and women—greedy, jealous, and above all quarrelsome. Trouble among mortals was often brought about by the quarrels and rivalries of the gods.

Now at this marriage feast Eris, the goddess of strife and discord, threw down a golden apple, on which were inscribed three words: FOR THE FAIREST. It was immediately claimed by three goddesses, each of whom thought herself the most beautiful: Hera, the wife of Zeus, chief among the gods; Athene, goddess of war, and Aphrodite, goddess of love. The three goddesses agreed to have a contest, of which Paris, the most handsome of mortal men, was to be judge.

When the goddesses appeared in front of Paris, Hera whispered in his ear, telling him that, if he would award her the prize, she would give him greatness and power. Athene promised him success in battle, and Aphrodite told him that, if he would award her the golden apple, she would give him the most beautiful woman in the world. Paris gave the prize to Aphrodite, goddess of love, and with her help he carried off Helen, wife of Menelaus, King of Sparta, while her husband was away.

Paris was the son of Priam, King of Troy, and his wife,

Hecuba. It was to Troy, a strong and wealthy city near the mouth of the Black Sea, that Paris took Helen, who was a demigod and the daughter of Zeus and Leda. She had been sought in marriage by the principal kings and chieftains of Greece. At the suggestion of Odysseus she was allowed to make her own choice. She had chosen Menelaus, and all the other princes had sworn an oath to defend him. So, when Helen was carried off to Troy, Menelaus appealed for help to the chief of the Greek Kings, his brother, Agamemnon. He at once promised to gather together an army and sail to Troy to demand the return of Helen.

The neighbouring princes all sent ships to Troy and besieged the city. So strong were its defences and so valiant its defenders, that the siege lasted ten long years.

Many and bitter were the battles that were fought on the windy plains between the city and the sea. Many were the brave men, princes and soldiers, on both sides, who were slain by the sword and never again beheld their native shores. But the city would not yield. So grèat was the pride of the Trojan lords that they would not make Paris give up Helen.

In the tenth year the Greeks got into the city by cunning. They pretended to be abandoning the siege and sailing away in their ships. They left behind a huge wooden horse, which the Trojans thought was an offering to the gods. They foolishly dragged it into the city. They did not know that it was hollow, and that inside it were armed Greek warriors. These warriors came out of the horse at dead of night, opened the gates of the city and let in the Greek army. The sleeping Trojans were taken by surprise, but they fought bravely. The battle raged all night long, and the Greeks set fire to the city, burning its houses and palaces and sending its towers toppling in flames into the streets. Troy was burnt to the ground. Its people were killed or taken into slavery. Some managed to escape by land or in ships.

Menelaus got back his Queen, Helen, and returned with her to Sparta. The Greeks embarked in their ships, laden with the precious things they had looted from the burning city. Agamemnon and the princes sailed for home.

Among the Greek heroes none was more resourceful than Odysseus. He was wise in counsel, cool and tactful. He was courageous in battle, energetic and cunning. He had been one of the Greek leaders shut up in the wooden horse. He had been one of the suitors of Helen, but when she chose Menelaus for a husband and went to live in Sparta, Odysseus married Penelope, taking her back to his rocky island of Ithaca. She bore him a son, Telemachus. But then the war began, and for ten years Odysseus had not seen his wife, his son and his home. He had brought a fleet of twelve ships to the war, and as soon as it was over, he ordered his men to sail for home. He had one thought in his mind—to leave Troy far behind him and find again the island he had so long dreamed of.

eric fraser

PART I: THE VOYAGE

1

The Lotus-eaters—the Cyclopes

War

WHEN THE LONG siege of Troy was over and the city destroyed, Odysseus gathered together his followers and their twelve ships and set sail. The siege had lasted for ten years, and Odysseus longed to go home to his wife Penelope and his son Telemachus in the palace on the far-off rocky island of Ithaca. But the winds were against him, and the voyage was long. First he was driven towards the shore at Ismarus, and here he and his men landed and laid waste the city. Then they plundered the whole country, in order to fill their ships with food and wine. The inhabitants, the Cicones, had fled inland, but they returned with others, who gathered thick as leaves in autumn and prepared to drive out Odysseus and his men. With their bronze spears and shields they did battle against Odysseus, killing many of his men. Towards evening Odysseus saw that the battle was lost, so he and his men fled in their curved ships and left the land of the Cicones. Because Zeus, chief among the gods, sent a wind from the north, they were driven southward.

The wind was so strong that the men were forced to haul down the sails and take to the oars. For nine days they were driven off their course and could in no way row towards Ithaca. On the tenth day they set foot on the land of the lotus-eaters, so called because they were content to dream away their lives eating the sweet, delicious fruit of the lotus. Three of Odysseus' men were sent to spy out the land. They were received peacefully and hospitably by the inhabitants, who gave them some of the fruit of the lotus. Such was the effect of the lotus upon the minds of the three men that it acted like a drug: they had no desire to sail away and find their homeland once more, but wished to stay among the lotus-eaters for the rest of their lives. Odysseus sent a strong party to find the three men. They were bound and put in the bottom of his ship, while the rest of the company rowed away with all the speed they could.

Over the grey sea sped the curved ships, until at last the land of the Cyclopes came in sight. These were a strange race of men, each having one eye only, set in the middle of his forehead. They lived upon the flesh of sheep and goats and the cheese which they made from their milk. They neither ploughed the land nor sowed seed, but ate of the corn and fruit which grew in abundance, for the soil was very rich and the weather warm and sunny. Grapes grew in plenty on the vines, so that they had all the wine they could drink. Each man lived for himself and his family in the natural caves in the mountain side, and they were without laws or government.

Just off the shore of the Cyclopes' land was a small, uninhabited island where goats ranged freely and where the rich soil was untilled by the hand of man. It had a natural harbour, and here the ships of Odysseus put in at dead of night. Next morning the men went out with bows and spears and brought back goats for food. They had on board plenty of wine, most of it stolen from the Cicones of Ismarus; so they spent the day resting and feasting. As they rested, they gazed across to where the fires of the Cyclopes sent their smoke up into the clear blue air. Next day Odysseus ordered eleven of his ships to stay where they were in harbour, while he took his own ship to the Cyclopes' shore to discover what manner of people they were. He and his men landed, and not far from the shore they discovered a cave whose entrance was surrounded by a stockade of trees and stones. Over it were stretched branches of laurels to keep off the sun and rain. Now this was a cave where lived a solitary giant Cyclops named Polyphemus. He was less like a man than a great mountain peak. Inside the stockade under the leafy shelter he kept his sheep and goats at night. Odysseus left all his ship's company beside the shore except for twelve picked men, and with these he set out to explore the giant's cave. He took with him a goatskin full of strong, sweet wine as a peace-offering for the inhabitant of the cave. He entered the stockade, looked round and found that no one was there; so he and his men went further inside and entered the cave. It was full of great baskets of cheese and vessels full of skim milk; there were also wooden pens for animals.

Odysseus' men were alarmed at the boldness of their leader and urged him to take some of the cheese and as many sheep as they could and return to the ship. But Odysseus refused, wishing to see what kind of man inhabited the cave. They made a fire and on it threw a burnt offering to the gods who protected them. Then they had a meal of cheese and awaited the return of Polyphemus. At dusk the men heard a great stamping and shuffling as the giant came in, bearing a huge

B

pile of logs. This he flung to the ground with such a
crash that the men all started back in terror and fled to
the darkest recesses of the cave. They peered out to get
a sight of the mountainous figure of the giant, who
next went back to the mouth of the cave and drove in
his bleating herds. Then he seized a huge stone
boulder and blocked up the entrance to the cave.
Odysseus and his men were prisoners. Polyphemus
then let his animals suckle their young, keeping back
some of the milk to make cheese and some for his
supper.

When he had done this, the giant looked round the
cave and saw Odysseus and his men. With a roar like
that of thunder rolling round the mountains he said:

"What men are you? Why do you come here? Are
you traders or are you pirates?"

The men were terrified, but Odysseus stood bravely
in front of the monster, gazing up into his one eye and
replied:

"Sir, we are neither traders nor pirates. We are
sailors on our way home. In the name of the gods
who look down upon all men alike, we crave your
hospitality. We ask for shelter until our departure and
then for gifts from you, as is the due of strangers
upon your territory."

"You are a fool," answered Polyphemus, roaring
with laughter. "I do not believe in your gods and I
set no store by them. If you are sailors, where is
your ship?"

Odysseus, not willing to put himself at the mercy
of the monster, craftily answered:

"We have no ship. As we reached land, Poseidon,
master of the sea, broke up our vessel, and we were
left to struggle to land as best we might."

Then the giant, without further reply, did a horrible thing. He strode forward, seized two of Odysseus' men and dashed out their brains on the wall of the cave. Then he cut up their bodies and threw them aside for his supper. He took no further notice of Odysseus and his terrified followers, who, the blood frozen in their veins, could only look on as he gorged himself upon the flesh and bones of their dead companions. Then Polyphemus lay down and was soon fast asleep. It would have been easy for Odysseus to kill the giant with his sword, but he had seen the great boulder that blocked the entrance to the cave, and he knew that he and his ten men had not the strength to move it. So he ordered them to lie down and sleep as best they could.

Next morning Polyphemus sat up, stretched his great hairy shoulders, yawned and got to his feet. He milked his sheep and goats once more and again confronted the men cowering at the back of the cave. His arms shot out and he grasped two more of their shrinking forms. Serving them just as he had served their comrades the night before, he made his breakfast of their mutilated bodies. Never had there been a more horrible sight than that of this cannibal at his work. Wiping the blood from his lips with the back of his shaggy forearm, he drove his flocks out of the cave and rolled back the boulder. Odysseus and his men were prisoners, and alone. The leader said to his eight followers:

"Be of good heart, my men. Terrible as has been the fate that has befallen your comrades, we are yet safe, and I will think of a way to get out of here alive."

Looking about him, Odysseus found a great stake of pinewood, which he told his men to hack down to a

length of seven or eight feet. While some of them cut
one end of the stake to a sharp point, others blew up
the embers of the fire until they glowed hot and bright.
Then the point of the stake was twirled in the heart
of the fire until it was as hard as iron. Then Odysseus
ordered his men to hide the weapon under a heap of
dung at the back of the cave. Next he chose four of
his men to plunge the stake into the giant's eye when
next he lay asleep.

That evening Polyphemus returned to the cave,
driving his flocks before him. He replaced the boulder
and set to work milking the goats and letting the ewes
suckle their young. Then Odysseus was forced to look
on while the monster seized yet another pair of his
ill-fated crew and dashed them to pieces. He had now
only six men left.

"This cannibal," he vowed to himself, "will get no
more of my friends if I have my way tonight."

When Polyphemus had gorged himself upon the two
bodies, Odysseus brought him a bowl of the strongest
and sweetest wine he had taken at Ismarus. This was
the wine he had brought in a goatskin from his ship.
It was so strong that men were not used to drinking
it before first mixing it with a great quantity of water.

"Now that you have finished your meal," Odysseus
said, "will you not try some of my wine? Perhaps it
will move you to pity, and you will let us go."

The Cyclops seized the bowl and greedily swallowed
the strong liquor at one gulp, smacking his slobbery
lips as he did so.

"More!" he said, thrusting the bowl back into
Odysseus' hands. "It is good—far better than the wine
of my country."

Polyphemus drank three bowls in this way. Then,

besotted with wine and hardly able to stand upright, he asked Odysseus his name.

The crafty Odysseus answered: "My name is Noman."

"Your wine is good, Noman, and in gratitude I will give you the gift you ask. My gift to you will be that I will eat you last. I will let you live until all your followers are dead."

With these words the loathsome cannibal tottered to the ground and fell at once into a deep sleep, snoring heavily. At once Odysseus made his men blow up the fire and heat the pointed end of the stake.

"Courage, my friends," Odysseus said. "Our trials will soon be over. You four, take up this weapon, two each side, and I will lay hold on the end of it. We will stand behind our enemy, and when I give the word, we will ram it into his one eye with all our force. Then take care to scatter to the corners of the cave and avoid his fury."

They stood at the giant's head and raised the stake aloft.

"Now!" cried Odysseus, and they brought it down with all their might. There was a searing, sizzling sound as the giant was blinded, and at once he gave the terrible howl of a wounded beast, leaping to his feet and pulling the stake from his eye. Then he stumbled to the mouth of the cave and shouted up through the laurel covering:

"Help, friends! Help me. They are killing me."

So thunderous was the voice of Polyphemus that a number of Cyclopes came running to the cave and cried:

"What is the matter, Polyphemus?"

"I am being killed," answered Polyphemus.

"Who is killing you?" asked the Cyclopes.

"Noman is killing me," cried Polyphemus. "Noman is my enemy. I am being killed by trickery."

"Then if No Man has attacked you," said one of the Cyclopes, "you are in no need of help. You have had a nightmare. Some god has sent you a sickness. Zeus, father of the gods, has sent this sickness on you as a punishment for some misdeed. You must pray to your own father, Poseidon, lord of the sea. When you have done this, go back to sleep and trouble us no more."

So the Cyclopes left the cave of Polyphemus, and Odysseus laughed in triumph.

When the giant had recovered somewhat from his pain, he staggered blindly to the mouth of the cave, pulled away the boulder and sat with his arms outstretched to catch anyone who tried to get past him. Odysseus continued to plan his escape. He and his men must somehow get past the huge monster at the entrance. He drew a number of long willow branches or withies from a heap at one side of the cave and tied the rams together in threes. Then he made each of his six men crawl under the bellies of the rams, clinging upside down to the fleeces of the ram in the middle. Then he bound them to the animals with more of the withies, so that they could not let go and drop to the ground. He next chose a single, very fleecy ram for himself and clung on underneath. The rams then began to make their own way out of the cave in search of pasture. As they did so, Polyphemus felt along their backs, not knowing that Odysseus' men were underneath. Odysseus himself, clinging to the belly of the last ram, followed the others. As he did so, Polyphemus spoke to the ram and said:

"Ah, if only you could speak. Then you could tell me where this Noman is who struck out my eye."

But Odysseus passed safely out of the cave and immediately dropped to the ground, ran to his companions and unbound them. They drove the rams down to the ship, and Odysseus told the men on board to take them in and stow them away for food. Great was the rejoicing of the men to see their six companions once more, and great was their sorrow at hearing of the fate of the others. Odysseus told them to lose no time in weeping, but to take up their oars and row and row as hard as they could away from the Cyclopes' shore. As they did so, Odysseus could not refrain from standing up on the deck of the curved ship and calling out in exultation to the stricken Polyphemus.

"Cannibal giant," he shouted, "you have had your just reward. Nevermore shall you insult innocent wayfarers and abuse the laws of hospitality as laid down by Zeus, who is master of us all."

For answer Polyphemus, who was standing on a rock facing the sea, tore off a huge boulder and hurled it with all his might towards the ship. With a terrifying crash the boulder came down just in front of the ship and drove it back to land. At once Odysseus seized a long pole and pushed the ship away from the shore, shouting to his men to row for all they were worth. Once more Odysseus stood on the deck, preparing to defy Polyphemus. In vain his men tried to restrain him.

"Say no more, master," they begged, "but let us get away from this place without more danger. If he hears your voice, he may easily throw more rocks at us and sink the ship."

But Odysseus did not heed them.

"If any man asks who blinded you, Cyclops," cried Odysseus, "tell him it was none other than Odysseus, sacker of cities and son of Laertes, King of Ithaca."

When he heard these words, Polyphemus groaned in agony.

"Now I see," he said, "that the fate has befallen me that was foretold by a soothsayer who once lived among us. He told me that I would be destroyed by the mighty Odysseus. I supposed this Odysseus to be a great hero and a warrior, but now I see that he is a puny, cunning dwarf who has triumphed over me with wine and trickery. Come on shore, Odysseus, that I may now receive you as befits a hero and the son of a king."

But Odysseus refused, and Polyphemus knelt on the ground and raised his hands in prayer.

"O Poseidon," he cried, "if, as you say, you are

truly my father, let me be avenged on Odysseus, son of Laertes. May he never be allowed to return home. But if he is destined to do so, let him pass through danger and hardship and lose all his companions. Let him return alone to find sorrow in his house."

Then the giant rose to his feet, seized another mighty rock in his arms and hurled it at the ship. But it struck the sea behind, so that the ship was driven on. It was beached on the deserted off-shore island where Odysseus and his men joined their companions in the other ships. They divided the rams among the crews, and offered one as a sacrifice to Zeus in order to ward off the curse spoken by Polyphemus against Odysseus and his homecoming. But Zeus, as it fell out, did not heed Odysseus' sacrifice and was already devising ways to torment him further. The companions feasted and went to sleep for the night. In the morning they sailed away, stricken at heart for the loss of their fellows.

which parts did you like best? why?

2

Aeolus—the Laestrygonians—Circe

AFTER THEY HAD left behind them the land of the Cyclopes, Odysseus and his companions came to the floating island of Aeolus. It was surrounded by a high wall of shining bronze which rose straight out of the blue sea. King Aeolus had six sons and six daughters who lived together on the island and spent much of their time in feasting. Odysseus was made welcome and entertained kindly by the King and his children. For a month they stayed there, telling of the Trojan War and the end of that great city, and of the adventures that had befallen them since their departure.

Now Aeolus had been put in charge of the winds by the gods. When the time came for Odysseus to sail away—for he was longing to continue his journey home—he asked the King for his help and his blessing. Aeolus gave him a sack made from the hide of a nine-year-old ox. Then he imprisoned the winds inside this sack and stowed it in the hold of Odysseus' black ship. He bound it to the timbers of the ship with a strong silver cord. Then, after bidding farewell to his guests, Aeolus sent forth the West Wind, which bore the ships away from the island.

"Now at last," Odysseus said to himself, "I shall see once more my home and behold the beloved form of my wife Penelope."

His wish almost came true, for the ship fared so well and the wind was so favourable that after nine days the rocky peaks of Ithaca could be seen in the distance. Indeed, the keener-sighted of the men said they could even make out the forms of men on the shore. But before they came any closer, Odysseus was so weary that he fell asleep.

This was the moment for his men to whisper together.

"Our leader has stuffed his ship full of precious things from Troy," said one of them. "Now King Aeolus has given him yet another bag full of treasures. Let us open it and see what presents he has won."

So they untied the silver cord and loosened the leather thongs at the neck of the bag. At once all the winds escaped and there was a violent storm. The ship was caught up in a whirlwind and tossed hither and thither. The island of Ithaca disappeared in the tempest, and in tears and desperation they were driven further and further from their home.

The violence of the ship's motion awakened Odysseus, and when he saw what had happened, he cursed the sailors and was tempted to throw himself overboard in sheer despair. Then he regained his courage and determined to press on with even more resolution than before. Nothing but death should prevent him reaching his homeland.

An easterly wind now drove them back to the bronze-girdled island of Aeolus. They landed and refreshed themselves on shore with food and wine from the ships. Odysseus took a herald and went to greet the King.

The King and the princes came out of the palace and were amazed to see Odysseus again so soon.

"How has it come about," he asked, "that you are once more in this country? By now you should have been in Ithaca."

Odysseus almost wept as he explained what had happened. Aeolus looked alarmed.

"It is now clear to me," he said, frowning, "that you are accursed of the gods. This will bring us misfortune if you remain here. Begone, I command you, with all speed."

When they left the island of Aeolus for the second time, there was no wind at all, so the men had to smite the calm waters with their oars until they were weary as well as heavy-hearted. After six days of this labour they reached the country of the Laestrygonians. Here there was a large and hospitable harbour, and into it sailed all Odysseus' twelve ships except his own. The cunning leader kept his own vessel just outside the harbour, mooring it to a rock with a stout cable. Then he sent three of his men ashore to spy out the land and discover what sort of people the Laestrygonians were.

Anxiously Odysseus awaited the return of the scouts. Before long they came running back and leapt aboard the ship in a state of wild disarray, their eyes staring in horror. But there were only two of them.

"What has happened?" asked their leader. "Where is your companion?"

"Oh, master," said one of the two, "we were met by a maiden drawing water at a spring. She offered us hospitality, and we entered the house of her parents. Her mother was no gracious lady, but a horrible creature, ugly and fat. Then her father came in, a ferocious and brutal man. He raised his axe and, before our fellow could defend himself, struck off his head. He said the man would do for his supper. Master, we have come once more among cannibals.''

The cannibal with the axe was named Antiphates. As soon as he had killed Odysseus' follower and seen the others escape, he had rushed into the market-place and called his countrymen together, bidding them bring their weapons and attack the foreigners. At once a great army of the Laestrygonians ran to the harbour, howling and screaming. They at once attacked the eleven ships that were moored there. They flung stones and rocks, hurling spears and javelins at the almost defenceless sailors. The ships were smashed; some of the men dived into the harbour; others were killed. The Laestrygonians bore their bodies ashore in triumph.

Seeing that he could do nothing to help his un-fortunate men who had so rashly entered the harbour, Odysseus took his sharp sword and cut the cable by which his own ship was moored. He shouted to the crew to jump to their oars and drive the ship with all their strength away from the accursed island. In this way he lost all his ships except one. His men rowed on weeping and mourning for their lost companions until they came to the island of Aeaea, where lived the goddess Circe.

They beached the ship and spent two days resting and lamenting their lost comrades. They made sacrifices to the gods and prayed for deliverance. Then Odysseus went cautiously inland and climbed a steep slope. At the top of this he gazed across the green country, and beyond a thick wood he saw the smoke rising from Circe's palace. Then a graceful, horned creature trotted out of the wood and came to drink at the stream where Odysseus had stopped.

"Some god," said he to himself, "has sent me this stag to be our food."

He aimed his spear and killed the stag at one blow. Then he made a rope of withies and bound together the four legs of the stag. With the help of his spear, he took up the animal and made his way back to the ship. The ship's company rejoiced at their leader's safe return. They prepared the stag and spent the day feasting upon its flesh and drinking wine from their store.

Next morning, when dawn touched the skies with her rosy fingers, they arose, and Odysseus addressed his company and told them to be of good courage. Next he divided them into two equal parties, of which he took charge of one, making Eurylochus leader of the other. They drew lots, and the lot fell upon Eurylochus. So he and twenty-two of the men set off to explore the country and find out what went on at the palace. As they emerged from the wood, they saw the palace in the midst of a level clearing. Around it roamed wolves and lions. Now Circe, being an enchantress, had tamed the animals with drugs so that they did not attack the men, but fawned upon them— patting them with their forepaws and licking their hands. But the men were frightened.

Then from the inside of the palace came the sound of a woman's sweet voice, singing as she sat at her weaving. One of the company, by name Polites, said to his comrades:

"There is some fair woman in this palace. Let us call out to her and beg for her help. Perhaps she will be hospitable to us as strangers."

As the men called out, Circe came to the door of the palace and courteously invited them in. All entered except their leader Eurylochus, whose cautious suspicion kept him outside. He feared treachery from the fair goddess. The servants arranged chairs on either side of a long table and brought cheese and barley meal. Bowls of wine were provided, but these had been drugged by the enchantress so as to send her guests to sleep. The men fell greedily upon the food and wine. Presently their heads began to nod, sinking lower and lower on their breasts. As soon as they were asleep, Circe sprang lightly from one to the other, touching each with her wand. Then she drove them to the sties where the swine were housed. Each man had the bristling snout, ears and body of a pig, but they still had the minds of men. When they were fully awake once more. Circe fed them upon acorns and beechnuts, which they eagerly devoured, snorting and snuffling as they did so.

Eurylochus returned sorrowfully to the ship, hardly able to speak for his tears. He had not seen everything, but only the disappearance of the men into the palace, whence they had not returned. He felt sure that evil had befallen them.

At once Odysseus girded on his sword and told Eurylochus to guide him back to the palace. Eurylochus drew back in horror:

"Mighty Odysseus," he begged, "do not go to that accursed place. Let us board the ship and get away from this place as fast as we can."

"No," said Odysseus stoutly. "You stay here, if you dare not go with me. Take charge of the ship while I go and discover what has become of your unfortunate comrades."

Looking warily round on all sides, the leader approached the palace in the clearing. Just as he was emerging from the wood, he was met by Hermes, the messenger of the gods, disguised as a countryman. He warned Odysseus of the fate of those who had been turned into swine.

"The same fate is intended for you," he said. "But I am sent by the gods to save you from it."

He stooped to the ground and pulled up a plant. This was the herb moly, whose root is black and whose leaves are milky white.

"Eat this," said Hermes, "and it will protect you against the enchantress's drugs. Now listen to what else you must do."

After giving him instructions, Hermes left Odysseus, who went on his way to the palace. At the gates he called to Circe and she came out and courteously invited him in.

"Sit here, stranger," she said in her soft, wheedling voice. "You must be in need of refreshment. Here is a bowl of wine."

Odysseus drank deeply, but the drug had no effect because he had eaten the moly. Circe smote him with her wand and said:

"Now get you to the sty and lie down among your swinish friends."

Instantly Odysseus did as Hermes had instructed him. He drew his sharp sword and laid it against the throat of the goddess. She dropped to her knees and begged for mercy.

"Who are you, stranger?" she asked with trembling lips. "What is your name, and whence come you? You are the only man who has ever drunk of my potion and not felt its effect. You must be Odysseus, son of Laertes. Yes, I was warned by Hermes, messenger of the gods, that you would come this way as you journeyed home after the war at Troy Put away your sword, and let us make love."

"How can I make love," (said Odysseus scornfully,) "to one who has turned my friends into swine) Swear that you will do no more harm to me, or I will kill you with this sword."

Circe swore as he had ordered her and he sheathed his sword. Then her servants bathed Odysseus, and she gave him a gorgeous mantle and led him to a richly-furnished hall. Here a feast was provided, but Odysseus had no wish for food, so heavy was his heart at the fate of his company.

"Why do you not eat and drink, handsome stranger?" Circe asked gently. "Why do you look so sorrowful? Are you afraid that I will do you more mischief? Have I not sworn to you a sacred oath?"

"Before I can eat and drink," Odysseus answered sternly, "you must set my men free."

Obediently Circe went straight to the sty with a new charm and restored the men to their human shape. Indeed, they looked younger and even more handsome than before. Then she led them into the palace, and great was their joy to see their leader again.

"Stay here with me," begged the goddess. "You must be weary with long voyaging, and to live in this delightful island will restore your strength."

So Odysseus went down to the ship and greeted Eurylochus and the rest of his men. They flocked about him, telling him that to see him once more was like returning to their homes.

"Tell us of our companions," they said. "Are they safe and well?"

For answer Odysseus told them to draw the curved ship further up the beach and stow their treasures for

c

safety in a dry, hollow cave. Then they were to come to the palace and see their comrades feasting. But the faint-hearted Eurylochus turned to the men and spoke:

"Do not go with him to this accursed place. Do you not remember what happened when you followed him into the cave of the Cyclops? Be cautious for your lives, and do not run into more danger."

Odysseus was so angry at the disloyalty of his follower that he almost slew him. But the others spoke soothing words and said:

"We will come with you, Odysseus, but let us leave Eurylochus behind to watch over the ship."

"Oh, do not leave me," begged Eurylochus. "I am afraid to be alone."

So together they all went to the palace of Circe, where they found that the goddess was treating the men like princes. She had given them rich and delicate foods and provided each with a splendid robe.

Then when the newcomers had been entertained in the same fashion, Circe turned to Odysseus and said:

"I know all about your adventures and the hardships you have undergone since you left Troy. You are wasted and thin. Stay here with me. Eat, drink, rest and grow fat, until you are ready to take your leave and be on your homeward way."

Odysseus consented, having no more fear of the goddess's enchantments. And for a whole year he and his men stayed on the island, feasting, drinking, hunting and making sport.

But even pleasures can become wearisome, and at last the men came to Odysseus and said:

"Prince Odysseus, for a whole year we have been here. Is it not time we were going home to our wives and children? It is many years since we set eyes on our own houses and sat by our own hearths."

Odysseus agreed, and went to Circe to ask her to let them go, as she had promised.

"By all means," Circe answered. "But your way home will not be easy. You must first go to Hades, the dread underworld, where reigns Persephone, the cruel queen of the dead. There you must speak to the blind prophet Tiresias, who alone knows everything of the fates and fortunes of mortal men."

"But how can we enter Hades?" asked Odysseus. "No mortal man has ever been there before and come away alive."

Circe told him to listen carefully while she instructed him how to visit Hades in safety and consult the prophet. Then she gave him a rich and many-coloured robe, and herself put on a cloak of gold set with gleaming gems. She ordered her servants to put food and wine and precious gifts on board his black ship. Then the men hoisted sail, bent their backs to the oars and steered the ship away from the harbour. Circe and her followers gazed after them until the ship was out of sight.

3

Odysseus visits Hades

WHEN THEY HAD left the island of Circe behind, Odysseus and his companions sailed over the blue waves with a fair wind following. The sails were stretched tight above the deck of the black ship, and the sun shone to gladden the hearts of men. But Odysseus was thoughtful; his mind was full of forebodings of the terrible journey he was to make. Hades was that dark underworld where all men go when they die, but it had never before been given to any living man to journey there and return to the shining fields of day.

From morning till night the ship fared on. As the sun went down beyond the western rim of the sea, they reached the edge of the world and the River Oceanus which encircles it. As daylight died, they came to the country of the Cimmerians, a land of perpetual shadow where the sun never shines. Here Odysseus, remembering the instructions of the enchantress Circe, beached the ship. Then he made two of his companions, Perimedes and Eurylochus, bring ashore two sheep. He himself carried wine and mead in leather skins, and a bag of white meal. Slung at his belt was his sharp sword, and over his shoulder he bore a spade. With this he dug a trench. It was a cubit wide and a cubit long, as Circe had

ordered. Into it Odysseus poured his offerings to the
dead—mead, sweet wine and water. On top he
sprinkled the white meal, praying to the spirits of the
dead. He promised them that on his return to his
native land he would make them sacrifices, and
especially that he would offer a black ram to the spirit
of the prophet Tiresias.

Next he bade his companions hold their two sheep
in front of him. Taking out his sharp sword, he
cut the animals' throats and let the blood flow into the
trench. At this the spirits of the dead trooped out
from the depths of Hades and stood about him—brides
and youths yet unwed, old men, some of them full
of wickedness, tender maidens with grief yet fresh at
heart, and others wounded or slain in battle by bronze
spears, clad still in their bloody armour. As they
gathered about the trench, they wailed so sorrowfully
that Odysseus' heart was frozen in fear. Nevertheless,
he kept firmly in mind the instructions given him by
Circe. First he ordered his two companions to skin
the sheep and burn their flesh as a sacrifice to the
dead. Then he held his sword over the trench to
keep off the thirsting spirits of the dead until he had
spoken with Tiresias.

Among the first of the dead to appear before
Odysseus was his mother Anticleia. It was a shock to
see her for she had been alive when he had left home
to go to Troy, and he had not heard of her death.
But she did not recognise her son, and Odysseus wept.
Much as he longed to speak with her, he did not, for
he was impatient to see Tiresias.

It was not long before he saw the blind prophet
from Thebes holding a golden sceptre in his hand.
He it was who knew all that went on among living

men and could foretell what things would befall them.

"Odysseus, son of Laertes," he said, for he knew without sight what man stood at the trench, "What is it that brings you to the dark halls of the dead? Take away your sword, so that I may drink of the blood and speak truth to you."

Odysseus did as he was commanded. Tiresias drank of the sheep's blood and spoke.

"You desire to know," he said in his slow and solemn voice, "how you may reach your home. You will not achieve this without great hardship and trouble because you have an enemy among the gods. This is Poseidon, the earth-shaker and lord of the seas. He wishes to punish you for the blinding of his son Polyphemus, the Cyclops. Nevertheless, you will in the end reach sea-girt Ithaca in spite of all his power and malice. You will do this on one condition. Listen carefully. You will reach the island of Thrinacia in the midst of its sea of violet blue. On this island graze the sacred cattle of the sun god, Helios. On no account let your men kill or capture any of these animals. Leave these cattle unharmed and you will reach home in the end despite many hardships. If, however, any harm comes to the sacred beasts, you will lose your ship and all your men. You will reach home alone and in the ship of strangers, only to find misery, danger and near ruin in your own palace and among your own people. As for your final end, you will die at sea after a long and calm old age."

"Prophet Tiresias," said Odysseus when he had heard these words, "I will remember all you have said, for no doubt you have divine foreknowledge of my fate. But tell me one thing more. How may I be known and recognised by my mother Anticleia?"

"This I will tell you," replied the prophet. "You must let her drink of the blood in the trench. Any of the spirits of the dead whom you allow to partake of the blood will tell you the truth."

With this Tiresias departed, and Odysseus saw him no more.

Then Odysseus stood by the trench until his mother stooped and drank of the blood. She looked into his eyes and spoke.

"Dear son," said she, "How is it that you come to be among the dead? Between the living and the dead are great streams of which the greatest is Oceanus. Have you come here on your way home from Troy? Have you not yet seen your wife and child?"

"It is as you say," Odysseus answered. "I have not seen Greek soil since I sailed from Troy after the burning of that great city. I have not set foot upon my native Ithaca. But tell me, my mother, how you came to die. Tell me of your husband, my father Laertes, and of my son Telemachus. Most of all, I would know how it fares with my wife Penelope. Has she been faithful to me, or has she taken another husband in despair at my long absence?"

"Your wife," answered Anticleia, "remains steadfast. All day she weeps in her palace at your long absence. Your son lives his life in peace, and is well received by all. Your father Laertes lives amidst his fields, and does not go down into the town. He wears sorry clothes, like the toilers in the fields. He has no rich bedding, but lies at night amidst the ashes of his hearth. Old age is heavy upon him, and he weeps continually for your absence. As for me, it was not through long illness that I died, but through grief on your account, and through the loss of your affection and your sympathy. O my son, I died for love of you."

Three times Odysseus stretched out his arms and would have embraced her, and three times, spirit as she was, she avoided his embrace.

"O mother why may I not embrace you?"

"I am one of the dead, my son," answered his mother. "I am but a spirit with no body for your arms to embrace. You cannot touch me. Leave now the shadowy halls of death, home of us spirits, and journey back into the sunlight."

She flitted silently away, and the cruel Queen Persephone sent forth the wives and daughters of great heroes that they might drink of the blood in the trench. Some spoke to Odysseus, telling him of the brave men they would see no more. He spoke also to many of the warriors and heroes of old. He spoke to Agamemnon, King of all the Greeks and begged him to say how he had died.

"I was slain", said he, "by my fierce wife, Clytemnestra. Yours, Odysseus, is of a gentler kind, and will never harm you."

Then the King asked Odysseus if he could tell him of the fate of his son Orestes, but Odysseus said he had no knowledge of what became of any of the Greeks after they had left Troy.

Next there appeared the spirit of Achilles, greatest among the heroes. So sad was his countenance that Odysseus tried to console him.

"Great were you among the warriors," he told him, "and now you are great among the dead."

"I would rather be the meanest of slaves than greatest among heroes," replied Achilles, "if only I were alive on earth. Can you tell me anything of my son Neoptolemus?"

Odysseus told the hero that his son was a very brave youth, that he had been inside the horse at Troy, and that he had escaped unwounded. More than that he could not say.

Many other spirits did Odysseus see and speak to. Some of them were those who had done evil deeds upon earth. One was Tantalus, condemned to perpetual hunger and thirst. He stood at the edge of a stream which receded from him when he approached it, and beneath trees bearing all manner of delicious fruit. But when he reached up to take it, the wind swept the branches out of his reach. There too was Sisyphus, condemned to roll a heavy stone up a hill. Each time he neared the top, the stone rolled back to the bottom so that his punishment was never-ending.

Other mighty heroes, such as Heracles and Jason, appeared to Odysseus' wondering eyes. Still others he hoped to see, like great Theseus, but the shades of the dead thronged round him in such great numbers, wailing and grieving, that fear took hold of him. So Odysseus retraced his steps and went back to where his men were awaiting him in the curved ship. Once on board, he looked back with terror at the dark shores of Hades, where ruled the King of the dead and his cruel Queen Persephone. Then at a command from him, the crew bent to the oars and swung the ship away from the mouth of the River Oceanus. Before long they were once more in the sunlit land of the living. A breeze sprang up, and they shipped their oars and hoisted sail. As they sped over the wine-dark sea, Odysseus kept in his heart the words of the blind prophet Tiresias.

4

The Sirens—Scylla & Charybdis— the Golden Cattle of the Sun

THE SHIP MADE speed over the waves and was soon back at the island of the enchantress Circe. She arrayed herself in fine clothes and came down to the shore to greet Odysseus. Her maidens came with her, bearing food and wine for the men. Odysseus went to the palace and told Circe of his visit to the underworld and of the shades of the dead whom he had seen and spoken to.

"It is given to few men," she said, "to visit twice the abode of the dead. You are a brave man, and you deserve to succeed in your desire to reach your home again and to sit by your own hearth in Ithaca. You have more dangers to meet—dangers even more terrible than those that have already beset you.

"You must first pass the island of the Sirens from which none returns alive. These maidens sit in green meadows stretching down to the shore. They comb their gold tresses and sing their strange, haunting songs. They lure rash mariners to their perilous coast, and among the flowery meadows where they sit you will see the whitening bones of men who have died there. No man who hears them sing can resist the longing to leap from his ship and swim ashore. What you must do is this: as soon as the island comes into sight, put wax into the ears of all your men so that they can hear nothing. Let not the wax be removed until you are well past the danger. If you yourself, their leader, wish to hear this marvellous singing, have yourself bound with strong cords to the mast of your ship. Tell your men that, if you ask them to untie you, they are to save you by tying yet more cords around your body and the ship's mast. Do you understand?"

"Yes," replied Odysseus. "I will do exactly as you say." Circe went on:

"Next you must pass between two awful dangers. On one side is a giant, craggy rock whose towering head is lost in an everlasting dark cloud. In its side is a deep cave in which dwells the monster Scylla, who barks perpetually like a litter of hounds, eager for the blood of men. She has twelve dangling legs which are lost in the bottom of the cave; she has likewise six long necks, on each of which is a head, terrible to look on, having three rows of close-ranged, knife-sharp teeth. With these heads, which she twists and turns about on their writhing necks, she fishes for dolphins and other denizens of the sea. No ship ever passes without losing some of its crew to this ravening monster.

On the other side of the passage along which you must steer is a rock from whose side grows a great fig tree. Below it lives Charybdis, who is a mighty whirlpool. Three times a day she draws in huge quantities of sea-water, and three times a day she spouts it out, so that the sea all about is turbulent and the rocks are sprayed with white foam. You must not sail near this whirlpool while the sea is being sucked in, for no ship is able to keep from being drawn in and dashed to pieces. It is wiser to steer near Scylla, losing perhaps six of your men rather than that the

whole ship and all its company should be sucked down
by Charybdis."

Odysseus looked troubled.

"But if I lose some of my men to Scylla," he said,
"and pass safely by Charybdis, how may I return and
be avenged on the six-headed beast?"

"Scylla is no earthly creature," answered Circe.
"She is immortal and not to be fought with. The
wisest course is flight. If you return and attack her,
she will only seize and devour yet more of your men.
Fly you must. It is your only course."

"Next," Circe continued, "you will come to the
island of Thrinacia, where graze the sacred cattle of
the sun god Helios. There are seven herds, each of
fifty cows and bulls, and seven flocks, each of fifty
sheep. As Tiresias warned you, you must on no
account lay hands on any of these creatures. They
are immortal, having nothing to do with either birth
or death, and they are tended by fair-haired maidens,
the daughters of Helios and Neaera. If you leave these
herds and flocks unharmed, you may in the end
reach home; but if you harm any of them, you will lose
your ship and all your men; if you yourself return
home, it will be with much sadness, hardship and
bitterness of heart."

Odysseus listened gravely to the words of the
enchantress. In the morning, when rosy-fingered dawn
appeared in the east, he made his way to the ship.
Circe gave him provisions for their voyage; meat and
wine. The men sat in order on their benches and
smote the grey sea with their oars. When they were
clear of the land, Circe sent them a fair breeze so
that the ship needed only the spreading sails and the
hand of the helmsman to steer her over the water.

Soon they reached the island of the Sirens whose flowery meadows they could discern beyond a line of white breakers. Then the wind ceased and they were becalmed. They took down the sails and stowed them away. Then they bent their backs and began to whiten the waters with the tips of their polished pine oars. With the help of the hot sun and his own strong hands Odysseus melted a quantity of wax and made plugs which he had the men fasten firmly into their ears. Before doing this, he instructed them to tie him firmly to the mast and to refuse his orders to loosen him till the danger was past, however hard he should entreat them. He stood facing the shore with his back against the mast and they bound strong ropes about his body, tying them in knots behind his back. Then they smote the sea with their oars and drew nearer to the Sirens' coast. With straining eyes they saw the beauty of the maidens and the stark whiteness of the skulls and bones that lay strewn among the flowers and the gold-green grass. When the Sirens saw the ship, they raised their voices in a strange and overmastering chant, which only the ears of Odysseus heard. That is what they sang:

Hither, come hither, famed Odysseus,
Great glory of all the Greeks,
Draw up your dark ship upon our coast
And harken as we sing.
None has ever sailed his ship past our shore
Until he has heard the honey-sweet melody of our lips
And gone on his way wiser than when he came.
For we have knowledge of all things,
Of all that passed in the land of Troy
In the war between the Trojans and the Greeks;
All this we know, and we can tell too
Of all things that will happen upon the fruitful earth.

So piercingly sweet was the song of the false Sirens that Odysseus strained to break the bonds that bound him to the ship's mast. His muscles writhed and sweat poured from his body, which he longed to cool by plunging over the side of the ship and swimming to land. Had he done so, he would have stayed among the Sirens until his bones were whitened by the sun and salt wind. In vain he shouted to his men to untie him, calling them base wretches to disobey his commands. He shouted himself hoarse, till they could hear his words through the wax that filled their ears. Two of his men, Perimedes and Eurylochus, left their oars and took cords and bound him still tighter to the mast, though Odysseus cursed them as they did so. The crew rowed harder than ever, and before long the Sirens' music had faded from the air, and the vision of their flowery fields was faint in the distance. Then the men took the wax from their ears and untied Odysseus.

The leader stood up on the deck and said to his men:

"Be prepared for more dangers sent by the immortal gods. Be of good heart, strive onwards, and in the end you shall greet once more the wives and children whom you left behind when you came to fight at Troy. Remember whose wit and whose courage delivered you from the hands of the Cyclopes. With my help you will be delivered from our next danger and live to look back on this day with pride and thankfulness. We are approaching a deadly whirlpool, the white spray from which you can see on the horizon. Row manfully; and you, helmsman, keep the prow of the ship well away from that side of the channel."

But the cunning Odysseus said nothing of the danger that awaited them on the other side—the monster Scylla; for he was afraid that, if they knew of her, fear would overcome them and they would all be lost.

Odysseus buckled on his armour, grasped a long lance in each hand and took up his position on the prow of the ship. He strained his eyes to catch sight of Scylla, but he saw no sign of the grisly monster. The channel narrowed and, with fear in their hearts as they gazed at the boiling whirlpool, the men drove the ship towards the narrows between the two beetling rocks. The whirlpool was then pouring out a deluge of foaming water, and the men were almost paralysed with fright as they thought of the fate that would be theirs if this flood engulfed the ship. But in their fear and confusion they saw nothing of the other danger to which they were being steered, for the helmsman did as Odysseus had told him and kept the boat as far from the whirlpool as he could. So none

but fearless Odysseus at the prow saw the body of
Scylla rise out of her cave and bend her terrible
heads towards the ship. With a snarling cry, she
seized six of the men in her deadly jaws and dragged
them from the ship. Odysseus was helpless to save
them. The most piteous thing that ever he saw in all
his travels was these six men, writhing and screaming,
as the monster bore them down into her dark cave.
Never would he forget the screams of their final agony.

With terror and despair in their hearts as they
thought of their lost comrades, the men forced the
ship out of the strait, and before long they were making
westward to the pleasant island of Thrinacia. Odysseus
strained both eyes and ears; before long he saw the
golden cattle straying peacefully among the rich
pastures of the island. He heard their contented lowing
and the bleating of the sheep. He turned and spoke to
his men.

"We are coming," he said, "to the land where live
the sacred cattle belonging to the sun god Helios. I
have been warned strictly, both by the blind prophet
Tiresias and by the enchantress Circe, that on no
account must we lay a finger on these cattle. If we do,
the sun god will be angry with us and will call upon
Zeus, greatest among the gods, to punish us so that we
shall never again see our native shore. Keep clear of
this island, then, and drive the ship safely past it. Do
as I bid you, men."

At this there was a murmuring among the crew—a
murmuring of anger and discontent. They felt that
their leader was asking too much of them. Eurylochus
spoke.

"Odysseus, son of Laertes," he said, "You are a man
of iron, but we are weak and weary with the journey.

We are in despair at the terrible fate of our six comrades and we are worn out with straining at the oars and the ropes. Have pity on us and do not order us to leave this fair island behind. Night is coming on. Night is the time of storms, and we have no strength to battle with any sudden tempest that may be sent by the gods. All we ask is that we be allowed to beach our ship and enjoy a good meal and a night's sleep. You cannot grudge us this, for we have earned it. Then, as soon as dawn breaks in the east, we will willingly man the oars and the sails and leave this island for ever. You cannot be deaf to our pleading, great leader of men and King of Ithaca."

At this speech, all the men cheered and added their voices to that of Eurylochus. Odysseus saw that it was useless to argue, but his heart was heavy, for then he knew that some plot against him was being hatched among the gods.

"Very well, men," he said, "We will do as you wish. But before you go ashore, will you all swear a solemn oath that, if you come upon any bulls, cows or sheep, you will not touch them, but treat them as sacred to the gods?"

This they readily agreed to, and after the oath was sworn by every man, they drove the ship into an inlet where they tied her up near a spring of sweet water. They went ashore and prepared supper from the meat and wine that Circe had given them. After they had feasted, they began lamenting over their lost comrades until at last they fell asleep.

Towards dawn the gods sent a change in the weather. The wind blew, and the sky was filled with clouds and rain. They feared the ship might be dashed to pieces in the harbour so they ran down to

D

her and pulled her ashore. There could be no question of sailing away from Thrinacia until the weather changed once more.

But fortune was against Odysseus. For a whole month the wind blew and storms raged about the island. The men were forced to remain there, and every day Odysseus warned them not to hurt a single one of the sacred cattle. Before long they had eaten all the meat given them by Circe, and they were obliged to live on corn, oil and wine. They went inland with hooks and spears to catch whatever birds and wild game they could. Some ventured into the rough sea to catch fish. Before long there was no more corn and oil, and all they had to eat was such fish and game as they could catch. Odysseus was full of anxiety as he saw some of the men eyeing the peaceful cattle hungrily, so he went inland to the top of a hill to pray to the gods for help in getting away from the perilous island. He felt so weary that he lay down and slept.

Then Eurylochus gave the men evil advice.

"We are starving," he said, "and all we can look forward to is a slow and lingering death. There is not enough here to keep us alive, unless we kill some of these cattle. Let us risk doing that. We will sacrifice one of the bulls to Helios and beg him for forgiveness. If he does not forgive us, but sends a storm to wreck us on our homeward way, is that not a better death than slow starvation and the pangs of hunger? Death in a storm at sea will at least be quick."

The company agreed and, without delay, they drove the fattest of the cattle out of the grazing grounds and cut their throats. They skinned them and prepared a sacrifice to the gods. They took the fattest of the thighs and burnt them as an offering to Helios. Then they cut the rest of the meat into small pieces and put it on spits to roast it for their meal.

It was then that Odysseus awoke. Fearing some disaster, he hurried down towards the ship. It was not long before the sweet smell of roasting meat greeted his nostrils. He groaned aloud, guessing what had happened. It was not fish nor lean birds that smelt like this; it could only be good fat bull's flesh. At once Odysseus broke into prayer.

"Father Zeus," he groaned, "You have sent me sleep, and my men have defied my orders and offended your decree. Have mercy on us all, I beg."

The maidens whose task it was to tend the sacred cattle went at once to the god Helios and told him what had happened. Helios prayed to Zeus.

"Father of all," he cried in a loud voice, "Odysseus, son of Laertes, has killed the best of my sacred cattle. Be revenged upon him and his men, I beg you. If not, I will leave the haunts of men and hide my light in the dark halls of death, and the sun will no more shine upon the ways of men and ripen their crops and their grapes."

Zeus told the sun god to continue shining upon the earth and promised him to be revenged on the men for killing the golden cattle.

Odysseus had meanwhile rushed to where his followers were roasting the meat. The gods began to show signs of their displeasure. The skins twisted and writhed in the flames, and the roasting meat cried out with the voices of bulls, bellowing as if it were alive.

Nevertheless, for six days the men feasted on the stolen meat, and on the seventh day the month-old storm died down. The wind changed, the sky became calm and fair, and Odysseus ordered the crew to go on board and drive the ship away from the island.

But the anger of the gods is swift to punish the insolence of men. Scarcely had the black ship left the shores of Thrinacia when a heavy cloud appeared in the sky right above it. A sudden squall from the west hit the ship. The mast snapped before there was time to lower the sails. It fell upon the helmsman's head. His dead body rolled overboard. Then Zeus sent from the sky a thunderbolt, which hit the ship, smashing it into fragments and flinging every man into the sea. Helplessly they plunged and struggled round the ship, but could in no way save themselves. Odysseus was last to leave the ship. Before it sank he was able to lash together some planks and make himself a raft. To this he clung with all his strength and was borne on the waves away from the whirling remains of his ship.

Odysseus alone was saved. But his troubles were not by any means over. The wind changed, and his raft was carried back to the whirlpool Charybdis. He had no means of steering it away from the boiling cave at the foot of the rock, and was drawn helplessly towards it. A mighty waterspout separated him from his raft and flung him into the air. Clutching wildly, he managed to grasp at the fig-tree, whose spreading arms and roots stuck out high above the whirlpool. Almost ready to let go his hold out of sheer exhaustion, Odysseus stared down into the rush and spume of the water. At last his raft, which had been sucked down, came into sight, floating on the waves. At once he let go of the fig-tree and dropped down beside the raft. He scrambled on to it and lay there, gasping for breath. By the mercy of the gods he was able to keep out of reach of Scylla, the terrible six-headed monster and was swept past her towards the open sea. So for nine days he floated, without food or drink, and on the tenth day he was cast up on the island of Ogygia. Here dwelt the fair-haired nymph Calypso, who took Odysseus in and entertained him with kindness, giving him rest, food and fresh clothing.

prophecy had come true

5

The Gods in council—
Trouble in Ithaca

EN LONG YEARS had passed since the destruction
of Troy. All the Greek heroes who had not
perished in that war had returned home—all
except Odysseus. He alone ate out his heart in sorrow
in the island of Ogygia, hospitably entertained by the
nymph Calypso. She wished to keep him there, for
she loved to hear of his manly exploits both at Troy
and on the wide seas. He had no means of escape, for
his ship had been smashed and his men were all dead.
Yet in his heart he did not wholly despair. Had not
the prophet Tiresias and the enchantress Circe both
foretold that he would one day reach home, in spite
of all his hardships and misadventures?

But men do not decide their own fates. They are
in the hands of the immortal gods who rule the
earth from their thrones on lofty Mount Olympus.
Great Zeus, chief among the gods, had already decided
that one day Odysseus should find his way home,
although Odysseus did not know what was in the mind
of the god. Indeed, all the gods were sorry for
Odysseus and felt that his trials had lasted long
enough. Only Poseidon, ruler of the seas, was
Odysseus' implacable enemy. Now it so happened that
this god had left Olympus to visit the limits of the
world, and farther shores of the great sea, ranging

its coasts from where the sun god Helios rises in the east to the place of his going down in the far west. While he was away, the other gods were sitting in the hall of Zeus on Mount Olympus talking of the destinies of men.

"Men blame us, the gods, for their unhappiness," said Zeus. "True, we are all powerful, but we do not bring ill fate upon men; it is their own blindness, folly and wickedness."

Then Athene, the grey-eyed goddess who had always been Odysseus' protector, spoke out.

"True, father Zeus," she said. "Many men deserve their fates, but Odysseus, the wise and strong, has suffered too much. My heart is torn for him, grieving on that distant island far from his home. The nymph Calypso keeps him there with her sweet, seductive words. But he longs only to go home and be with his wife Penelope, drinking the wine of comfort in his own halls. In his mind's eye is always the picture of the smoke rising from the fire in his own hearth. Will not all-powerful Zeus take pity on him? No man living has been more obedient to the gods and more dutiful in making sacrifice and offering prayers."

"You are right, Athene," answered Zeus. "I can never forget Odysseus, wisest of men. It is the anger of one god, Poseidon, which has kept him away from Ithaca all these years, for the sea god has never forgiven him for blinding his son Polyphemus the Cyclops. But it is time Poseidon's anger was abated, for one god cannot be allowed to have his way against all the rest. In spite of Poseidon's power the wise Odysseus must be allowed to go home."

Athene looked up at Zeus with grateful eyes, and then she glanced about her at the assembled gods.

"If such is our will," she said, "let Hermes, our winged messenger, fly down to Calypso's island and tell her of our decision. I myself will go to Ithaca and rouse Odysseus' only son Telemachus, now a brave and comely young man of twenty. He is in despair because the house of his father is overrun by princes and chiefs who hope to gain possession of the kingdom. I will hearten the young man against them. I will give him courage to defy these princes and tell them to be gone. Then I will send him to sandy Pylos and to Sparta to seek news of his father."

Then the assembly broke up, and Athene bound on the winged sandals with which she skimmed over mountain and plain, sea and island. With her bronze-tipped spear in her hand she alighted on sea-girt rocky Ithaca, where she disguised herself as Mentes, an old friend of Odysseus, for the gods do not appear to mortal men in their own shapes. She stood at the gate of Odysseus' palace which stands above the sea beside an inlet on the western shore.

As Athene looked through the gate, a sorry sight met her eyes—a scene of disorder and wildness such as the home of a great prince should never show. The stone courtyard was strewn with the hides of the pigs and goats that had been slaughtered to feed the unruly men who had invaded the palace. These called themselves suitors for the hand of the queen, Penelope. They told her she would never more see her husband and that she must regard herself as a widow. If she would only make up her mind to choose one of them for a husband, peace and order would be restored. But she would not listen to them, for in her sorrowing heart there yet lived the hope that Odysseus would come back. Inside the banqueting hall, a feast was being prepared. The squires and henchmen of the suitors were busy washing the tables down with sponges, mixing wine in silver bowls and slicing up great joints of roast meat. While the suitors lolled on the skins in the courtyard, gambling, jesting and playing draughts, Telemachus sat there too, apart from the rest. The young man was not tall, but he was well built and upstanding, with the long curling hair of his countrymen and dark, keen eyes. Just now he had a brooding look, and there was a frown on his brow. He surveyed the gambols of his guests with contempt and loathing.

"Why, oh why," he sighed, "is there no sign of the father I have scarcely seen? Is he alive or dead? Will he never return and drive away these scoundrels, for how can I do anything alone?"

Then this brow cleared and he rose to his feet. He had seen the grey-eyed stranger at his gates, a tall man in middle age with a bronze-tipped spear resting on the ground at his side. Telemachus took the man by the hand, greeted him courteously and led him into the hall. That it was no man he entertained but a goddess he could not know. He took the stranger's spear and put it in a stand of polished wood where stood the spears that Odysseus had left behind twenty years before. He placed a beautiful carved chair for the stranger in a quiet corner of the hall, and set a stool for himself beside it. Then as was the custom in that hospitable time, a maidservant brought a silver basin and a jug of water and washed the hands of the stranger. Another servant brought a low table laden with meat and bread of all kinds. Then Telemachus urged the goddess to take food and wine. The suitors put their dice and coins in their wallets and lounged into the hall, laughing and joking. They took their places at the long tables and fell to attacking the meat and wine which their servants had prepared.

When the feast was drawing to a close, they called upon the minstrel Phemius to entertain them with songs at his lyre.

Telemachus and Athene sat apart, seeming to take no note of the feasting princes, and talking in low tones so that they might not be overheard.

"My guests," Telemachus said bitterly, "may well jest and call for songs for they have not a care in the world. They eat and drink at the expense of another man. That man, my father, may be drowned in some far ocean, or his bones may be rotting on a desert coast, unseen by any but the wheeling seabirds. He is dead, I know. He will never return. But tell of yourself, stranger. Where do you come from? Is this the first time you have been to Ithaca, or are you by chance an old friend of my father? In former times his palace was famous for its hospitality, and he had many visitors."

"My name," replied the goddess, "is Mentes. Perhaps you have heard tell of me. I am an old friend of your family. I am on a journey to Cyprus, and I called in here for friendship's sake. If you wish to know more about me, ask your grandfather, Laertes. I hear that he never comes down to the city, but lives in the country among his swine and his crops. I had hoped to find your father here and it grieves me that he has been so long absent. But don't despair, young man. Something tells me that he will return— sooner, perhaps, than you dare to hope. If he were a free man, nothing would prevent his coming back. I feel sure he is held prisoner somewhere, perhaps on an island from which he cannot escape. Yet, escape he will. You may be sure of that. So you are his son," the goddess went on, gazing keenly at the young man. "I can see a likeness. You have the same dark eyes, full of wisdom, the same head set firmly on broad shoulders. You seem a worthy son to the hero of Troy. Now tell me, who are these men who make free of your house and shake the hall with their noise? Can they be guests, or is it some band of pirates who have broken in?"

"Stranger," Telemachus answered, "what you behold is the ruin of my house. My father will never return. These are chiefs and princes from other parts of Ithaca and from the neighbouring islands. They have come to demand the hand of my mother in marriage. Whichever of them wins her will win also all our treasure, our palace and our gold, and such of our flocks and herds as have not already been slain to satisfy their greed. They are eating us out of house and home. But my mother is steadfast. She will not answer them. When all our wealth is consumed, I shall die, and the house of Laertes and Odysseus will be destroyed and forgotten."

The goddess laid a comforting hand on the young man's shoulder and said:

"Ah, my friend, how sorely you need the strong arm and sharp spear of that great hero. I have not seen him these many years, but I know that, if he were standing unarmed in that doorway, these guzzling swine would be glad to creep away with their miserable lives.

"Now listen," continued the goddess in low tones, drawing still closer to Telemachus, "and I will tell you what to do. Call upon all these men to assemble tomorrow and command them to leave your house. If your mother wishes to marry, let her go back to her father's house and be married there. As for you, fit out a ship, the best you can, and man it with trusty sailors to take you to Pylos and to Sparta, to seek for news of your father. If you hear that he is yet living, return and endure these trials for one more year. But if you hear for certain that he is really dead, return and build him a funeral pyre. Pay him due reverence and sacrifice to the gods. Then give your mother in marriage to the worthiest of the lords. After that, you can at least be ruler in your own house."

Telemachus listened intently to all that Mentes told him. The goddess then rose and said:

"Farewell now, for I must be on my way. You have my blessing, and may the gifts of the gods be yours. You are a child no longer, but a grown man. You must speak and act like a man."

Telemachus begged Athene to stay, but she would not wait. The young man led her out of the hall and across the courtyard. When she was out of the gates, she paused for an instant and then turned herself into an eagle. Immediately she took wing and sped over the city and out to sea. Telemachus marvelled, for now he knew that his visitor was a god.

With all that she had told him ringing in his ears, he turned and went back among the suitors, fired with a new courage.

The minstrel, striking with his fingers the stretched cords of his instrument, now sang to the suitors the story of the war against Troy and its burning by the Greek warriors. Penelope, mother of Telemachus, had come down from her room and stood in the entrance to the hall. She was silent, and her face was veiled.

Under the veil she wept, for she had heard the song from her room. It grieved her so deeply that she came down to beg the minstrel to sing a different song.

"Phemius," she entreated in a low and earnest voice, "This song will break my heart, for it tells of those things through which I lost my dear lord, Odysseus. You know many other songs to delight the ears of men. Sing one of them, I beg."

"Mother," said Telemachus gravely, "let the minstrel sing what he will. All men love to hear new songs. Be brave, for it is father Zeus who sends all joy and sorrow as he will."

Penelope looked at her son with surprise, for now he spoke not as boy but as a man having authority. Silently she went upstairs, and Telemachus, taking advantage of the pause in the singing, spoke to the lords at his table:

"Let your feasting go on," he said, "and hearken to what songs you will. I too love to hear such a tale as this. But in the morning you must all assemble in the public square and listen to me, for I have something to say to you. I warn you now that I shall call upon you to leave my halls and enjoy your feasting somewhere else. If you deny me this, I shall pray solemnly to the gods to punish you for your offence against my house."

At this the princes marvelled, for they had never before heard such words from the young man of twenty. Some hung their heads in silent anger, and some bit their lips. Now the foremost of Penelope's wooers was Antinous. It was he who spoke first.

"Dear lord Telemachus," he said in the smooth tones of a dandy, "let me compliment you. These words of yours are inspired. It will be a hard day for us if ever you should rule as king in Ithaca."

"Antinous," replied Telemachus promptly, "if it pleases all-seeing Zeus to make me king in Ithaca, I will gladly rule here. But it may fall to another to become king. All I claim is the right to be sole ruler in my father's house."

It was now the turn of Eurymachus, another of the suitors, to speak.

"As you say, Telemachus," said he, "only the gods know who will rule in Ithaca. We are content that you should be master in your father's house. But who was the stranger who came to speak with you? Did he bring tidings of Odysseus?"

"Yes, tell us who the stranger was," said another. "He had a fine appearance, but he went before we had time to make his acquaintance."

Telemachus did not tell the princes that he knew his guest had been a god. All he said was:

"That man was Mentes, an old friend of my family. But I have no further news of my father."

He said no more, and when the singing and the revelry were over, and the lords were stretched out in drunken slumber, Telemachus went quietly to his own room and turned over in his heart all that the stranger had said to him. The old family servant Eurycleia went with him, carrying a lantern. She had been taken into the household as a slave long ago by Laertes, and had stayed with his family ever since. She had nursed Telemachus as a baby, and no one loved him more. Carefully she folded and laid aside his doublet of soft linen, and when she left him, he lay all night wrapped in his sheepskin. He thought of what Athene had told him to do next day, until sleep closed his eyes.

6

Telemachus and the suitors

AT DAWN TELEMACHUS arose and prepared to meet the assembled men of Ithaca. He buckled on his sandals and slung his sharp sword over his shoulder. He sent forth heralds to bid the assemble in the market-place. Then, accompanied by two swift hounds, he himself set out, and the goddess Athene, protector always to the house of Odysseus, shed upon him nobility and grace. He did not hurry, and by the time he had arrived at the market-place it was already crowded. The elderly lords made way from him as he took his place on the stone seat which had always been kept for his father. About him stood the elders, lords and men of importance. In the middle of the square crowded the common people, men and boys, some with dogs at their heels, which they tried to keep from quarrelling. A hush fell upon the assembly as an old, bearded lord rose to speak. This was Aegyptus. He had four grown sons. One of them had sailed with Odysseus and had been killed by the Cyclops. But Aegyptus did not know of his death. All he knew was that his son was lost and not likely to return. One of his other sons was a wooer of Penelope, and the other two remained at home on the farm.

"Men of Ithaca," said the old lord, "never since our King Odysseus departed for Troy twenty years ago

has there been a public assembly in this place. Now we
have been called together by his wise and noble son.
What can be the reason? Is it that there is news of our
king and his company?"

Telemachus rose to speak. A herald placed in his
hand a staff of peeled wood, the sign that he alone
had the right to speak.

"It was I who called together this assembly, and I
must say at once", he began, "that I have no news of
the expedition which sailed against Troy under my
father Odysseus."

At this there was a murmur of disappointment, but
Telemachus raised the staff for silence.

"I have to speak of my house," he went on. "Two
evils have befallen it. First, I have lost my father
Odysseus. Where he is, and whether alive or dead, only
the gods know. Secondly, my mother Penelope,
bereaved as she is, has been for many weary months
beset by a tribe of suitors, some of them the sons of
lords in this assembly. They were too cowardly to go
to her father Icarius and ask honourably for her hand
in marriage. Instead, they have invaded her house—*my*
house, fellow-countrymen—where they and their army
of squires and pages kill off our oxen, our swine and
sheep for their daily revels. They wash down their
meat with our dark wine, and all the substance of our
house is wasted. If great Odysseus were here, it would
be a different story; but I alone stand against them,
and I am weak and have little prowess in the fight.
Will not you, men of Ithaca, feel my wrongs as your
own and help me put them right? If you do not, the
gods will be revenged upon you for allowing this
scandal to take place in your midst. Did the wise and
gentle ruler, Odysseus, do you some evil, that you

allow his house to be used with such insolence? I appeal to you, in the name of Olympian Zeus, to be gone from my house and leave me to bear my bitter grief alone."

The young man's voice had risen to a nervous, high-pitched note, and, as he finished speaking, he flung the white staff on the ground before him, and tears burst from his shining eyes.

Except for the suitors, the men of Ithaca did not know Telemachus well, but they were deeply moved at the sight of the sturdy young man reduced to such angry hysteria. Pity filled their hearts and a great silence fell on the assembly. Even the dogs and the young children were still and quiet. Then Antinous, chief among the suitors, picked up the speaker's staff and addressed the young man. Most of the assembly could hear his smooth tones.

"Telemachus", he said, and his voice was like the thick honey that the countryman pours from the comb in summer to strengthen the wine, "why is it that you blame us, the wooers, for the ills of your house? The fault, if fault there is, lies with your mother, who—I speak with profound respect—is a cunning woman. For three years she has received us Greeks as suitors. She sends messages of encouragement to this man and that, so that we do not know where we stand. But she has no intention of taking any of us as her husband. Some time ago she invented a new device to ensnare us and try our patience. She set up a great loom in her hall, and on it all day she weaves a broad web. She addressed us in this way: 'Men of Ithaca and of Greece', she said, 'I beg you to be patient, eager as you are to speed on this marriage of mine. I am weaving a winding-sheet in which Laertes, father of

E

Odysseus, shall be buried when the fates come to call
him away to the dark halls of death. Do not press
me to choose one of you until this shroud is finished.
It is fitting that I should weave it with my own hands,
and if it were not so, the women of Greece would
think ill of me, for Laertes was a king and a ruler of
power and riches.'

"Thus spoke Penelope," Antinous went on, "and we
all agreed to her request. But listen well, young man,
while I tell you of your mother's cunning. Each day
she weaves her web, but each night she comes down
with her maidens, some bearing torches, and unweaves
what she wove during the day. So that her cloth gets
no longer, and we are put off continually. It was not
till recently that one of Penelope's maidens revealed
to us this secret. Now that your mother's trick has
been discovered, she has been obliged to finish the
weaving. At last, according to her promise, she must
choose one of us for a husband. It is your plain duty,
Telemachus, to see that she makes her choice. Your
mother is a woman of great beauty, wit and talent,
unequalled in the whole of Greece for her knowledge
of the household crafts and unrivalled for comeliness
by all the fair women of old, and even the goddesses
themselves. But in one thing she is foolish. She cannot
go on deceiving us for ever. So long as she continues
to put us off, we shall remain her guests. It is she,
not us, that is bringing about the ruin of your house."

"Antinous", said Telemachus, looking up into the
self-satisfied face of the older man, "you speak of the
woman who bore me and brought me up. I am her
only child, and the one person who has kept up her
courage and resolution during the twenty years of my
father's absence. He is away from home. Whether he is

alive or dead I cannot tell. I cannot send her back to
her father's house. To do so would disgrace me.
Besides, I would have to restore to Icarius her father,
all the gold, silver and other precious things he gave
her. This I cannot do, since the substance of our house
has been so much wasted these many years. Leave us
alone, my mother and me. Get out of my house. Go
and feed at the expense of others. How can you
expect that I alone should put up with the cost and
trouble of maintaining you and your unruly crew? If
I should send my mother away, I would invite the
certain vengeance of the gods against me. So get you
gone, or it will be upon you that the wrath of Olympian
Zeus and all the gods will fall."

For a few moments there was silence, and then, as
if in answer to the speech of Telemachus, Zeus sent
two eagles overhead. From the craggy summit of a
mountain they flew together; then they circled round
immediately over the market-place, glaring down
angrily at the men below. Then they fell to attacking
each other, tearing their flesh with beaks and talons.
Suddenly they ceased fighting and sped away to the
right, crossing over the city and disappearing out to
sea. At once there was a murmuring among the crowd.
Everyone marvelled what this sign should mean. Then
the great Halitherses, much skilled in the interpreta-
tion of omens, stood up and seized the speaker's staff.

"Silence, men of Ithaca!" he cried. "Listen to me.
Listen to me, especially you wooers, for it is clear to
me that a mighty woe is rolling down upon your heads.
Odysseus is not far off. Even now he is at hand, and
the seeds of death and of fate for you suitors have
already been sown and begin to take root. Not only
will the anger of the gods fall upon the suitors; it will

fall upon us all in Ithaca, even on those who do not
seek to wed the Queen. Let us men of Ithaca make
an end of the evil brought upon the house of Odysseus
by the wooers—or better still, let them end it
themselves. I do not prophesy without knowledge,
fellow countrymen. When Odysseus sailed for Troy, I
foretold—as some of you will remember—that in
twenty years he would return. That time has passed,
and his coming is at hand."

Then Eurymachus, a man of rough tongue, stepped
forward and without troubling to take the white stick
began to speak.

"Halitherses, old man", he said, "go home and
prophesy to your children, for they have cause to fear.
I am a better soothsayer than you. The birds of the
air are many. They fly hither and thither, but not all
are sent by the gods as signs and wonders. Odysseus
has perished at sea—you may depend on that. It is a

pity you have not done the same, old man. Then you would not be babbling prophesies encouraging Telemachus to defy us. Let me say this plainly: It is foolish of you to urge on the young man in such a way that evil will befall him. No doubt you do this to curry favour and win from him some rich reward. For your foolishness we, the men of Ithaca, will put a heavy fine upon you.

Let me speak directly to Telemachus", continued the rude-mouthed Eurymachus. "Listen to no drivelling soothsayer, young man, but do as we say. Send your mother home to her father and tell her to take one of us in wedlock. Her kinsfolk shall provide marriage gifts and a feast. If you and she will not agree to this, we shall continue to stay in your house and consume your substance. We defy you. You can do nothing against us."

By this time Telemachus' temper had calmed and he spoke quietly and with resolution, gazing at the uncouth suitor out of his dark eyes.

"Eurymachus," he said. "Enough of this. All that has been said here is in the knowledge of the gods, and they will send us all the destinies that await us. Provide me with a swift ship, and I will sail to Pylos and to Sparta for news of Odysseus. If I hear that he still lives, I will return and will endure your insults for another year. If I hear that he is dead, past all doubt, I will build him a funeral mound and give my mother in marriage to one of you."

Then Mentor spoke, he was a grave, elderly man into whose hands Odysseus had entrusted the safe-keeping of his house before he sailed for Troy.

"Men of Ithaca", he said, speaking bitter words in his clear, resonant voice, so that all eyes were turned to him, "Henceforth let no ruler be given to this kingdom who is not harsh and severe. Odysseus was kind and gentle, and see how his memory is treated. I blame the rest of you, who are far greater in numbers. Why do you not cry destruction upon the suitors? Shame upon you, men of Ithaca, for you do nothing."

Then Leocritus, one of the suitors, spoke.

"Mentor", said he with a sneer, "You are a fool. What is the use of your calling on the people to attack us? Of what use is resistance? Even if Odysseus himself were here, we are too many for him. Penelope would have no joy of his return, for he would meet his doom at the hands of so many warrior lords. Now let the people scatter to their homes, and let Mentor and Halitherses stay to help Telemachus on his journey. I prophesy that this voyage will not prosper."

The people left the market square and went off to their homes, while the wooers made their way back to the palace of Odysseus. But Telemachus did not go home. He walked down to the edge of the sea and washed his hands in the water. Then he prayed to his guardian goddess Athene.

"Hear me, O you who bade me prepare to go on a journey for news of my father. Help me, I beg, in my journey over the misty sea."

He turned round and saw that the old friend of his father was behind him. He did not know that Athene had taken on the form and voice of Mentor.

"Be strong", said the man's voice. "You are the true son of your great father, and through courage you will accomplish your purpose. Be brave and take no heed of the senseless words of the suitors who care nothing for the doom that awaits them. It shall be my charge to see that your voyage has a prosperous start, and I will myself go with you. Return to your home and see that jars of wine and skins full of barley meal are made ready. I myself will go into the town and choose out a stout and trusty crew. There are many ships in the havens about Ithaca. I will choose a suitable one, and together we will rig her and prepare for the journey."

With a heavy heart, yet uplifted by the words of the goddess, Telemachus went back to his house.

7

The journey of Telemachus

INSPIRED BY THE words of the goddess, but with a
heavy heart, Telemachus returned home. There he
found the suitors already flaying goats for the feast
and heating wine by plunging red-hot knives into it.
As the bowls hissed and steamed, the smooth Antinous
gave a laugh, strode up to the young man and clasped
him warmly by the hand.

"Speak no more words of anger, dear Telemachus",
he said, "Let your brow no longer be clouded by
displeasure, but come and join in our feast. Then we,
your friends, will see that a ship is fitted out so that
you may go in search of your father."

But Telemachus frowned even more darkly and
snatched his hand away from the older man.

"Antinous", he said, "is it nothing to you that, when
I was no more than a boy, you wasted my father's
substance and began the ruin of my house? I cannot
forgive you, and I cannot feast in your presence. I
cannot rest until I have brought about your ruin with
help from Pylos; I shall journey in a ship belonging
to another, for it seems that I am not to have one of
my own."

The suitors meanwhile were guzzling and swilling
wine. One young blood said with a sneer:

"This Telemachus is plotting our ruin. Perhaps he

will get help against us from Pylos or from Sparta. Perhaps he is going to some distant land to get poisonous herbs to put in our drink."

"Perhaps," said another youth with a laugh, raising his voice to make sure that Telemachus heard him, "the young man will fare like his father and be drowned. Then we should have to divide his goods between us and give his house, with his mother, to whomever of us can win her."

Telemachus ignored the insufferable swaggerer and went down to the vaults below the house. Here were stored gold and ornaments and rich clothing; sweet-smelling olive oil, grain and unmixed wine. The doors were always kept closed, and the old servant Eurycleia was on guard. Telemachus told her to fill twelve jars with the best wine and twenty well-sewn bags with barley meal.

"Do this secretly," he told her, "and see that the jars and bags are well guarded. I will come for them at night after my mother is asleep. I am making a journey to Pylos and Sparta for tidings of my father."

Eurycleia said, with tears in her eyes:

"You are the only child. What has come over you that you should want to sail over the wide seas? Your father is dead, I tell you. There is no doubt of that. The moment you are gone, those men will plot evil against you, to destroy you if you should return. They will steal all you have. Stay at home, I beg you, and live on your own lands."

"I must go, dear nurse", said Telemachus. "It is not my idea. It is a command from the gods. Tell my mother nothing of my departure until the eleventh or twelfth day or until she misses me. In this way we will not bring unnecessary suffering upon her."

So Eurycleia, shaking her head sadly, swore on oath that she would do as the young man ordered. Then, while he went off to join the suitors, she began to draw off the strong wine.

The grey-eyed Athene now took on the form and speech of Telemachus and went through the city speaking to all the men chosen to manage the ship which, in the likeness of Mentor, she had already chartered. The ship was moored at the far end of the harbour, and at dusk she told the sailors to gather on the quay and stow on board the tackle and rigging. Then she went to the house of Odysseus and sent sweet sleep down upon the carousing suitors and their servants, who rolled back on the skins, clutching their slopping winecups in their hands. Once more in the form of Mentor, the goddess spoke to Telemachus.

"Your company," she said, "are already waiting by the ship. Let us go without delay."

Together they went to the harbour where they found the long-haired youths awaiting them.

"Go swiftly to my house," said Telemachus to a number of the strongest among the men, "and bring the corn and the wine which my old servant will give you. She alone in my house knows of this voyage."

This was done, and when all was ready, Mentor and Telemachus got aboard and took their places at the stern. The last of the sailors to come aboard loosed the hawser, and with a favourable wind they put out to sea. As they left the shelter of the harbour, the sails swelled, and the ship sped out across the dark water. Then wine was mixed and poured upon the deck and on the surface of the sea as an offering to the gods, and especially to Athene, protectress of

Odysseus' house. All night long the curved ship made good speed over the surface of the deep.

On the sandy shore at Pylos stood the citadel of Neleus, father of the great wise Greek, Nestor, who now lived there in wealth and splendour. When the curved ship of Telemachus beached there, the people were sacrificing black bulls to the gods. Telemachus and Mentor were the first to disembark. Mentor told the young man to go straight to the citadel and greet Nestor. Telemachus asked how he should greet this great hero, a noted man among the warriors who had fought at Troy. Mentor, under whose guise still lived the goddess Athene, told him he would be inspired partly by his own thoughts and desires, partly by the goodwill of the gods.

Nestor was presiding at the council of the elders when Mentor and Telemachus appeared. Nestor and his sons rose and came forward to greet the strangers whom they invited to sit down among them and partake of the feast. Pisistratus, one of Nestor's sons, spread out fleecy skins for the guests to sit upon. He then ordered meat and drink for them, and offered Mentor a two-handled gold cup. He bade him drink in honour of Poseidon, for whom the feast was being held. Mentor did as he was bidden and handed on the cup to Telemachus who also drank. Then Mentor prayed to Poseidon to bring good fortune to Nestor, the giver of the feast, and to send prosperity and success to the venture which brought the strangers from Ithaca to the shores of Pylos.

When the feast was finished, Nestor rose and spoke to the guests. He was a broad and powerful figure, old and venerable, through whose grey, curling locks and beard the morning breezes strayed.

"Who are you, strangers?" he asked. "Whence do you come and whither do you go? Is it a trading venture, or have you some other mission?"

"Nestor", replied Telemachus, rising to his feet, "son of Neleus and glory of the Greeks. I will tell you who we are and why we have come. I am Telemachus, son of the great Odysseus, who sailed with you to Troy and was present at the sacking of that great city. I have heard much about the home-coming of yourself and other heroes, but I hear nothing of Odysseus. I believe that now, ten years after those events, my father must be dead. I wish to know the truth. Tell me, great Nestor, if you know anything about his fate. Do not, I implore you, soften the news out of pity for me."

All were once more seated, and Nestor spoke.

"Telemachus," he said, "You are welcome, especially since you are the son of my old comrade. You have come here to speak of sorrow, and so I will tell you of the Greeks and how they fared on the windy plains about Troy. Many heroes perished there—Achilles, Patroclus and one of my own beloved sons. But if you were to stay here for five years, I could not tell you of all the ills that befell us Greeks. It took us over nine years to finish the war. Among those who did most to bring about victory your father, the wise Odysseus, was one of the foremost. After the siege and the burning and pillage, I lost sight of your father. I saw nothing of him after he and his men had taken to their ships. As for me, I made good speed and finally came back to Pylos. I arrived here without knowledge of the other heroes. Later news began to reach me of some of them. I heard of the return of the Myrmidons, of Philoctetes and of Idomeneus, who returned in time to his native Crete."

Then Telemachus told Nestor of his own difficulties at home, recounting bitterly the actions of the riotous suitors and their efforts to win his mother in marriage.

Nestor looked grave and pulled at his white beard. "I have heard something of your difficulties," he said with a sigh. "Who can tell whether the mighty Odysseus will return and take vengeance upon these rogues? You have one hope: if the grey-eyed goddess Athene comes to your help, you may yet be saved from ruin. She was always the friend and protectress of Odysseus."

Beneath the appearance of Mentor, Athene smiled to herself, as Telemachus answered Nestor sadly:

"Alas, great Nestor, son of Neleus and companion of my father," he said, "I have lost all hope."

"Young man," said Mentor, "it is too soon to despair. If the gods are minded to bring a man home to his native hearth, they will."

"Mentor," replied Telemachus, "You do your best to comfort me, but my heart is filled with despair."

"I advise you", Nestor said, "not to remain here a day longer than you need. I grieve that I can give you no news of your father, but I will help you to continue your journey. Go at once to see Menelaus in Sparta. He has recently returned from a journey to a far country. He may have news to tell you. Depart by ship tomorrow, if you will; or if you prefer to go by land, I will furnish you with a chariot and swift horses, and my sons will go with you to show the way. Go and find the fair-haired Menelaus in Sparta. He will tell you the truth, for he is a man of knowledge and wisdom."

Mentor thanked Nestor for his hospitality and said that, before they parted for the night, sacrifices should

once more be made to the gods. This was done, and
the two guests prepared to return to their ship for the
night. But Nestor stopped them.

"You must not go back to your ship without gifts.
Let it never be said that a stranger came to the house
of Neleus and departed empty handed. I have fine rugs
and blankets, and of these I will make you presents."

To the amazement of all, Athene suddenly lost the
shape of Mentor and took on that of a sea eagle.
On wide-spreading wings she flew away towards the
harbour.

Nestor took the hand of Telemachus for fear the
young man was alarmed and said:

"Now you may have confidence; for be assured,
this was none other than Athene herself. In her
keeping you are safe."

Then the old man prayed to Athene and said he
would do her sacrifice in the hope that he would
bring good fortune to the house of Odysseus. A bed
was arranged for Telemachus, and the young man
Pisistratus was sent to rest in the same room. Nestor
and his other sons wished them goodnight and went
to their own quarters.

At dawn Nestor assembled with his sons to prepare
a sacrifice. A man was despatched to bring in a heifer,
and another messenger went down to Telemachus'
ship to invite all the company to a feast. A goldsmith
was sent for to adorn the horns of the heifer with
gold, and Athene herself came to be present at the
sacrifice in her honour. When all were assembled the
horns of the heifer were gilded, and the beast was
sacrificed with due solemnity. White meal and wine
were sprinkled on the beast as parts of it were burned.
Telemachus, meanwhile, was given water in which to

bathe himself, oil to anoint his body, and fine robes
to put on. He came forth looking like a god.

Swift horses were yoked under the shafts of a chariot
in which were placed jars of wine and leather sacks of
meal. When Telemachus had bidden farewell to the
great and hospitable Nestor, and the hero had wished
him good fortune, the young man climbed up into the
chariot. Pisistratus leapt up beside him and grasped
the reins. He touched the horses' flanks with a whip,
and soon they were speeding off across the plain. All
day they travelled, leaving behind them a cloud of
white dust. Then as darkness fell, they reached the
inland town of Pherae. Here they feasted and spent
the night in sleep. They were up early next morning
and set out before the sun had scarcely risen above
the far hills.

8
Telemachus at Sparta

ISISTRATUS, SON OF Nestor, with Telemachus beside him, drove the swift horses down into the wide plains of Sparta. Because of the breadth and openness of these plains Sparta was famous throughout Greece for its horses, and Telemachus marvelled as he watched the herds of graceful, fast-moving animals that grazed or sported in the fields. In Ithaca there were no horses, for the island was small and rocky, having no spaces for exercise.

At the palace of Menelaus, King of Sparta, a banquet was in progress to celebrate two weddings— that of Menelaus' daughter to a son of the great Achilles, and that of one of the sons of Menelaus to a Spartan maiden. The company sat feasting in the great hall, with the King at the centre. They listened to the sweet, wild strains of the ministrel, and watched with amusement the antics of a pair of acrobats who tumbled and wrestled on the floor. Then a page stepped up to Menelaus and told him that two strangers were at the door.

"Why did you not bid them come in?" asked the King.

"I did not know whether you would wish to entertain them," answered the page.

Menelaus frowned:

"No stranger shall ever be turned away from these doors," he said. "We ourselves have often been entertained on foreign shores. Ask the strangers to come in at once."

Telemachus and Pisistratus were led in by attendants who gave them water in which to bathe themselves after their hot and dusty journey, and new clothes to put on. Then they were brought into the banqueting hall. Room was made for the two strangers at the King's side. He welcomed them graciously and said:

"When you have satisfied your need for meat and wine, you must tell me who you are and where you come from. I can see that you come of noble blood."

As he spoke, he was looking keenly into Telemachus' dark eyes. The young men looked round the wide and lofty hall in wonder and admiration. It was hung with ornaments and trophies of great price and decorated with gold and silver so that it shone with a splendour recalling that of the starry skies.

Telemachus said in a low voice to Pisistratus:

"Look at the beauty of this palace, my friend. I never saw so much bronze and gold and ivory in all my life. Why, the palace of great Zeus on Mount Olympus can scarcely be more beautiful."

"My young friend," said Menelaus, who had overheard the words of Telemachus, "I am sure that no palace on earth, even the most sumptuous, can be compared with the halls of the gods. I am known to be rich, but I would give half my riches to restore to life those noble heroes who lost their lives fighting at Troy. Them we shall never see again. I think of them often as I sit here, and the tears fall from my eyes."

Telemachus was listening to the King with a

F

thumping heart and indrawn breath. Was he going to learn something of his father?

"I think of them all," Menelaus went on, "but the man I think of most and grieve for most sorely, is the godlike warrior Odysseus. He was first among all the Greeks in every exploit, being both courageous and prudent. Now we have no knowledge of whether he is alive or dead."

At these words Telemachus could no longer keep back his tears. He buried his face in the purple cloth of his tunic. As Menelaus watched him, he wondered if he should ask him who he was. But Queen Helen came into the hall, beautiful as the virgin goddess Artemis. All men caught their breath as she entered, and Telemachus raised his tear-filled eyes and gazed for the first time upon the fairest woman in the world. The golden-haired Helen, daughter of Zeus, was Menelaus' wife. She it was, whose beauty had brought about the ten years' siege and the doom of Troy. Her women placed for her a graceful stool and beside it stood a basket of blue-violet yarn, the same from which had been woven the tunic given to Telemachus. In Helen's hands they placed a golden distaff, on which she spun the yarn into thread.

"Who are our guests, Menelaus?" she asked, her keen eyes having already surveyed them. "Surely the one nearest you is the son of godlike Odysseus whom we knew so well in former days. It must be little Telemachus whom he left behind as a baby when he departed from Ithaca."

"He is indeed the very image of Odysseus," agreed her husband. "And when I mentioned Odysseus just now he covered his face and cried."

It was the turn of Pisistratus to speak.

"Great Menelaus," he said, "my companion is indeed the son of Odysseus. My father Nestor sent me with him as a guide. He has come here in search of help, for Odysseus has been long away from home, and Telemachus has none to aid or comfort him."

Menelaus turned to Telemachus, laid a kindly hand on his arm and said:

"Once more you are doubly welcome—first as a noble youth in your own right and secondly as the son of great Odysseus. None fought more resolutely in my cause than he. My debt to him can never be repaid."

With that he began to weep, and the fair-haired Helen wept too, and so did Pisistratus. All seemed overcome with ancient woes. Helen had been thinking how she might bring comfort. She rose from her stool, dried her eyes and went in search of precious herbs which had been brought from Egypt and kept in her store. She brought the herbs and stirred them into the

wine bowls as a means of bringing relief to pain and forgetfulness for sorrows too smartingly remembered.

"Attendant," she said, "bear this bowl round, and see that all drink of it. Whoever tastes it shall have no more sorrow this day. Yes, he would feel no grief, even if he were to see his own brother killed in battle."

Gracious Helen spoke words of encouragement to Telemachus and praised his noble father.

"You well know," she said, "how that war was started on my account—how Paris, son of Priam, King of Troy, captured me and carried me off to the city. You know how my husband's brother, Agamemnon, raised up a mighty army which sailed to Troy to recapture me. Now of all the princes who furnished ships and men for that expedition, none was wiser, braver or more cunning than your noble father. I shall never forget how one night he disguised himself as a beggar and came boldly into the walled city to spy out its defences. No one but I guessed who he was. As a beggar he came into our very palace. I questioned him as to who he was, but he turned my question aside. So I asked him into my own room and promised that I would not betray him. After all, was he not a Greek, and was I not a prisoner in the hands of the enemy? So he told me the Greek plans and then left the city. I alone knew he was a spy from the Greeks. I rejoiced to think how the Greeks were planning to take the city and carry me back to my dear husband."

"Yes," said Menelaus, taking his wife's hand, "and how well I remember his courage and resourcefulness as we lay inside the wooden horse, unsuspected by the Trojans who were all round us. You, my wife, walked round the wooden monster, softly murmuring our names, so that each of us could almost fancy it was his wife speaking. We might have answered you and given ourselves away, had not the cunning Odysseus laid his finger to his lips and forbidden us to utter a word."

So until nightfall, when it was time for sleep, they told tales of past woes and triumphs.

Next morning King Menelaus made Telemachus sit down beside him and tell him why he had journeyed to Sparta. So the young man told his host the whole story of the troubles that he had left behind him in Ithaca, how a band of riotous and greedy princes and chiefs were persecuting his mother, and feasting day and night upon his food and wine. He described their games and orgies, their drinking bouts far into the night, that turned the house of Odysseus into a tavern.

Menelaus exploded into anger, cursing the vile men who were so dishonouring the memory of such a great hero and making miserable his poor wife and his only son.

"The curse of the gods on such a pack of coward beasts!" he cried. "But they have made themselves a home in the den of a lion; and when the lion returns, he will destroy them. Now I will tell you, my young friend, all I know of Odysseus, as it was revealed to me by Proteus. He is the wizard of the ocean, the herdsman of Poseidon who looks after the seals that belong to the great sea-god. He knows the secrets of the deep. It so happened that on my return from Troy my ship was becalmed on the sandy coast of Egypt. Our food began to run short, and we were forced to wander up and down the beaches in search of fish. I was alone one day, and I must have been looking unusually miserable, for a sea-nymph took pity on me and offered to help me. She was, she said, the daughter of

Proteus, the magician. He would advise me, but first I had to capture him and hold him fast. This would be difficult, for he had the power to change his shape and so avoid my grasp. But it was absolutely essential that I should take him prisoner. Then he would answer my questions.

I fetched three of my companions, and we each dug for ourselves a hole in the sand, where we lay. The sea-nymph brought sealskins with which she covered us. Then the herd of seals, which had been playing and swimming in the waves, came out to lie along the beach; and about midday Proteus himself came from the water to count the seals. He lay down to rest, and when the heat of the midday sun had brought sleep to his eyes, I and my companions came out of our holes in the sand and seized him. Instantly he awoke, writhed furiously in our grasp and turned himself into a snarling lion. Next he became a sea serpent, so that we almost lost him in the water. But we hung on, and he turned into a fountain of clear water, and then into a many-branching tree. But we were too much for him. We would not let go, and in the end he took his own shape once more, that of the bearded sea magician, and said he was willing to answer my questions.

When I told him my ship would not move and asked what I should do to get it under way again, he said the gods were angry with me and I must calm their anger by making them sacrifices. Next he told me of the fate of the Greek warriors who had fought at Troy—how some had been lost at sea, and how some had returned joyfully home. He told me how my brother, the great Agamemnon, had been murdered as soon as he had landed in his own country. Finally he came to the hero Odysseus, King of Ithaca. 'He is yet living,' Proteus told me. 'He is yet living, but all his ships and his men are lost beneath the sea. He is a prisoner of the nymph Calypso on her island. There I saw him. He thinks only of his wife and his home, and tears fall from his eyes as he longs to return.'

That was the tale I heard from the old man of the sea," Menelaus concluded. "Then I made sacrifices to the gods, and especially to great Poseidon, lord of the ocean, and in time my ships sailed safely into the harbour here in Sparta."

Thus it was the King and Queen of Sparta received Telemachus in their palace, giving him new hope of one day seeing the father he did not remember.

In Ithaca, meanwhile, the suitors were talking among themselves about the flight of Telemachus.

"Unless we can get rid of this tiresome youth," said the smooth Antinous, "he may be troublesome to us. On his return he must pass through the narrow strait off Samos. I will take a swift ship and twenty good men and lie in wait for him. Then I can choose my time and take him prisoner."

But Medon the herald was eavesdropping. He heard the suitors' plot and at once went to inform Penelope. This was the first the Queen had heard of Telemachus' departure. She was overcome with grief and sat broken-hearted among her servants, lamenting. She rebuked them bitterly for not having told her. But Eurycleia spoke out and told her mistress that Telemachus had sworn her to secrecy with a solemn oath. Nothing was to be said to the Queen until eleven days had passed.

"You must pray to the goddess Athene, my child," Eurycleia said, "for it is not to be thought that the goddess will allow this ancient house to be utterly destroyed."

Penelope dried her tears and did as the old nurse had said. She prayed to Athene, and then passed the day alone in her room, thinking of her absent son and her lost husband. She begged the goddess not to allow the suitors' plot against Telemachus to succeed. Even as she remained alone on her bed, taking neither food nor drink, she heard faintly from below the riotous sounds made by the suitors as they lay at their day-long feast, the raucous laughter, the singing and the coarse jests.

Then in the dead of night, when the noise of the rioters was still, Penelope had a dream. Through the gates of sleep a faint vision appeared to her and spoke. It was her sister, who lived in a far country.

"You are troubled, my sister," said the vision, "but be comforted. Athene the goddess appeared to me and told me to speak to you. Have no fear for your son Telemachus. She watches over him and will not let harm befall him. She is sorry for you in your distress and told me to tell you this."

Penelope answered the dim ghost and said:

"Tell me also of my husband Odysseus. If you have had speech with immortal gods, you must be able to tell me also about my husband."

"Do not ask me," replied the vision, "for of Odysseus I have no knowledge."

Penelope would have said more, but the faint vision faded away and was seen no more. Day was breaking and the first notes of the birds sounded from the treetops. Penelope awoke, comforted by what she had learned about her son.

9

Odysseus leaves Calypso's isle

WHILE TELEMACHUS WAS preparing to sail home from Sparta and the suitors were plotting to destroy him, the gods were in council on Mount Olympus. The grey-eyed Athene spoke:

"O father Zeus, have you forgotten your servant Odysseus, eating out his heart in Calypso's island and longing to return to his faithful wife in his own country?"

"Have you not yourself planned, my daughter", answered Zeus, "that in the end Odysseus will return and take vengeance on the suitors? First, however, you must see that his son Telemachus makes a safe journey home and is not a victim of his enemies' plot. Go at once to Calypso, the fair-haired nymph," Zeus continued, turning to Hermes his messenger. "Tell her that at last she must part with Odysseus. He must build a raft and make a sail for it. Then in twenty days he will reach the land of the Sea Kings, who will speed him on his way back to Ithaca."

So Hermes made fast his golden sandals, took his staff and flew off over mountain and sea, skimming across the waves like a sea bird in search of fish. When he reached the island where Calypso had her cave, he found her alone, sitting at her loom and singing songs of joy and longing. A fire burned brightly in the cave, giving off a scent of burning cedar. Around the cave grew green, sweet-smelling trees where sang and chirruped all manner of birds. Over the mouth of the cave grew a luxuriant vine from which hung clusters of ripe grapes. Four springs of water fed four clear streams which wandered down through meadows of violets. Such a beautiful sight might charm the eyes even of a god who had seen all the wondrous sights earth could offer.

Calypso welcomed Hermes into her cave and gave him nectar and ambrosia, the wine and food of the immortals.

"What brings you here on your swift-winged feet?" she asked. "You visit me seldom. It must be something special which makes you my guest today."

"I come about the hero Odysseus," said Hermes. "Zeus has kept him for many years from his home and his people. Now he commands you to send him on his way without delay."

This message was like a knife in Calypso's heart.

"Alas!" she cried. "It was I who saved him when Zeus sent a thunderbolt and sank his ship. I have looked after him these many months, and he has been dear to me. But if it is the will of almighty Zeus that he leaves me, I will not hinder his departure. I have no ships and men, but I will tell him what you say. He must make his own way hence."

"Do this at once," Hermes answered, "for fear the gods may be angry."

Hermes rose and took his leave of the nymph and flew off from the island.

With a heavy heart the fair-haired Calypso went down to the shore where she found Odysseus weeping as he gazed across the lonely sea.

"Grieve no more, dear Odysseus," she said gently. "The gods have ordained that you must depart for your home. I will give you all possible help. You must make yourself a raft, and I will give you food and wine for the voyage, and a fair wind to carry you away from me."

Odysseus looked at the nymph in utter amazement, and refused to believe her until she swore an oath that she would not bring him disaster. She did this, and they went back to her cave, where they talked and feasted until nightfall.

Then Calypso said: "Odysseus, if you are resolved to leave me, you must. But there is hardship and suffering still in store for you. Why not stay here with me? I am a goddess, and I cannot think that your wife is as beautiful as I, who can give you all happiness."

"Goddess," answered Odysseus, "I know my wife Penelope cannot be your equal in grace and beauty. She will grow old, while you are immortal. Yet I am consumed with longing to see her and be at home again. To bring this about I would undergo another shipwreck and still greater hardships. I have borne many sorrows and can bear yet more."

In the morning Calypso gave Odysseus a great bronze axe, took him to the forest, and showed him where the strongest and straightest trees grew. She told him that, as she had no ships, he must build himself a raft. He set to work felling and smoothing the tall trunks and joining them together into a square. In four days he had finished the raft, fitting it with a rudder, a mast and a sail. It was launched on the water. On the fifth day, food and wine provided by Calypso was put on board. At last Odysseus took his leave of the nymph and set out with a glad heart.

For seventeen days and nights he had no sleep, but sailed his raft straight across the wine-dark sea, steering it at night by the stars. On the eighteenth day he had his first sight of land. On the horizon he could just make out the shadowy outlines of the island of the Sea Kings.

But even when the hero was so near land, his enemy caught sight of him. Poseidon, the sea god, was on his way back from a long journey, and when he caught sight of Odysseus, he was overcome by fury.

"The gods have changed their purpose", he said to himself, frowning, "while I have been away from Olympus. If I do not act now, this foolhardy voyager will reach land and be safe from my vengeance. Before that happens, he shall have trouble and sorrow as great as any he has known so far."

The god waved his trident in the air and gathered together the black, frightful clouds so that day was turned into night. At once the heart of Odysseus was struck by terror. So awful was the approaching storm that he felt sure he was doomed to die. He remembered Calypso's warning. He thought of the dangers and hardships he had overcome at Troy.

"Would god I had died with the heroes there," he said. "That would have been a noble death, but to drown alone will be shameful."

He could say no more, for at that moment a wave like a mountain burst over him and swept him from his raft. Dragged down by the weight of his sodden garments, he almost perished, but groping blindly, he felt for the raft, drew himself on to it by a mighty effort and clung there, breathless and gasping. The wind and the waves tossed the raft to and fro so that Odysseus would certainly have been dashed to his death if Ino, a sea-nymph, had not taken pity on him. She rose from the trough of a wave and sat on the end of the raft. "Unfortunate Odysseus," she said, "what have you done to make the remorseless Poseidon hate you so? But he shall not destroy you. Strip off your clothes and take this magic veil. Let go the raft and swim for land. Fasten this veil round your body and it will bear you up in the water. As soon as you reach land, loose it and throw it back into the sea."

Ino gave Odysseus the veil and slipped off the end of the raft into the tossing waves where he saw her no more. Odysseus was afraid, and wondered if this was a trick to make him leave his raft and be lost in the water. He decided to cling to it as long as it held together. As he was thinking this thought, a giant wave fell upon the raft and flung its timbers into the air, as the wind scatters a heap of straw. When the wave had subsided, Odysseus was left sitting astride a single log. He did as the sea-nymph had told him, stripping off his waterlogged garments and tying the veil about his body. He swam with all his strength, and the goddess Athene bound up all the winds except the one which would take him towards the shore.

For two days and two nights Odysseus swam on, helped by the strong wind; on the third day the wind dropped, and Odysseus saw that he was within reach of land. At first his heart was filled with joy, but when he looked closer, terror seized him. For there was nothing in front of him but sheer cliffs and jagged rocks.

Poseidon had not finished sending new torments upon his enemy.

"Have I swum all this way and cannot find a landing-place?" said the unlucky Odysseus. "If I swim along the shore in search of a cove or a beach, will not the current bear me out to sea once more? Or perhaps Poseidon will send one of his sea monsters to devour me."

But there was no help for it. Swim he must, and as he did so he saw that the cliffs became lower and the rocks gave way to smooth boulders. He reached the mouth of a river. As Odysseus felt the fresh water current of the river, he prayed to its god and begged him to deliver him from the anger of Poseidon. At last Odysseus staggered up the river-bank and fell senseless to the ground, gasping for breath. When he came to his senses he remembered the command of the sea-nymph, unwound the veil from his body and cast it far into the sea. Ino rose, caught it and drew it beneath the waves. Then Odysseus wondered what to do next. If he lay down by the river, he might die in the cold and frost of the night; if he went inland, wild beasts might destroy him. He left the river-bank and went a short distance up the hillside. Here he found two bushes which had grown so close together that they formed a natural shelter, out of the wind and out of sight of men or beasts. He crept between the bushes and made himself a bed of fallen leaves; he lay down and pulled more leaves over him as a covering. Then the goddess Athene who had watched him through all his trials, sent sweet sleep to bring him relief from pain and fatigue.

While brave Odysseus slept long and deeply after his labours, his protectress, the grey-eyed Athene, went up to the palace of Alcinous, chief of the Sea Kings. She appeared in a dream to his daughter, the fair Nausicaa, who was asleep with her maidens in her richly adorned chamber. Athene appeared in the form of one of Nausicaa's friends.

"You are soon to be married," she said, "yet how careless you are of the fine clothes your mother and father have given you. They will not be ready for your betrothal day, and your parents will be ashamed. Early tomorrow you and your maidens must take your clothes down to the river and wash them. Ask your father for two mules and a cart, for the way is long and the burden heavy."

The dream faded as Athene left the palace of Alcinous and returned to her home in Olympus. At dawn Nausicaa awoke, full of wonder at her dream. She went through the palace and found her mother and father.

"Father," said Nausicaa. "There is much good linen lying about the house, crumpled and soiled. It is a fine morning, and I would like to take it down to the river to wash it; may I please have the use of two mules and a wagon?"

Alcinous agreed gladly to his daughter's request, and she and her maidens loaded all the soiled clothes on to the wagon. Her mother meanwhile prepared wine and olive oil and food, and this too was put on the wagon. Then Nausicaa mounted, with her maidens beside her, touched the mules with her whip, and they started off for the river.

The Princess and the girls unloaded the linen at the river's edge and set to work to wash it thoroughly. Then they rinsed it and laid it out to dry on the pebbles which had been washed clean by the tide and dried in the morning sun. They washed themselves and rubbed oil into their bodies and sat down to have their food and wine. Afterwards they played ball.

It was at this moment that Athene had planned that Odysseus should awake. He stirred beneath his covering of dead leaves under the two bushes. Hearing a girl's cry, he awoke. The ball had fallen into the water, and the cry of the maidens came to the ears of Odysseus.

"Where am I? What land is this?" he said, springing to his feet and brushing the leaves from his body. "What voices do I hear? Are they the voices of water-nymphs or of mortal maidens? I must find out."

He broke off a leafy bough to cover his nakedness and stepped out into the open. As soon as they caught sight of Odysseus, all shaggy and covered with sea salt, the maidens took fright and ran to the end of the beach. Only Nausicaa stayed where she was, for Athene had given her courage.

Odysseus approached the Princess and spoke to her gently.

"Fair lady," he said, "if you are an immortal, you must be Artemis herself. But if you are a mortal maiden, how happy must your parents be to have so beautiful a daughter. I am a stranger and in need of help. Give me, I beg you, some covering for my body and tell me how I may find the ruler of this country, that I may beg aid from him."

"Stranger," answered Nausicaa, "you seem brave, wise and courteous. I will give you all you ask. This is the island of the Sea Kings, and I am the daughter of their ruler, Alcinous."

Then she ordered her timid maidens to greet the stranger kindly, to give him means to bathe himself, and food and wine for his refreshment. They brought him clean, soft garments and olive oil in a flask. When he had bathed and anointed himself and put on the clothes, he looked like a god, and Nausicaa wished in her heart that he would stay on the island and be her husband.

10

Odysseus and the Sea Kings

W HEN ODYSSEUS HAD finished eating and drinking, Nausicaa spoke to him.
"Let us go to the city, stranger," she said.
"I will take you to my father's palace. As we go
through the fields, follow close behind me. But when
we come to the city, you must be careful. You will
see the walls and the harbour and the market square,
through which you must pass. Among our people, I
fear, are some rude men who will look with curiosity
at a handsome stranger. They will know you are not
of this country, and would wonder what I was doing
in your presence, when it is thought that I must
choose a husband from among our own people.

This is what you must do. On the way you will
find a grove sacred to Athene. There, there are poplar
trees and a clear-running spring. Stay there until you
think that I and my maidens have had time to reach
home. Then go into the city and ask for the house
of Alcinous. You will have no trouble in finding it.
When you reach it, go straight in to where my mother
spins her sea-blue yarn at the fireside; my father sits
there beside her, drinking his wine. Greet my mother
courteously, for, if you win her favour, you will the
sooner reach your home."

Nausicaa climbed into the wagon, touched the mules

G

with her whip, and they began to move through the fields towards the city. At sundown they came to the grove of Athene. Here Odysseus bade the Princess farewell; and when the wagon was out of sight, he prayed to the goddess Athene and begged her to help him win favour in the eyes of the Sea Kings, so that they might help him to get home. Athene heard the prayer of Odysseus.

Nausicaa reached home, and her brother unyoked the mules and carried in the clean linen. The Princess was greeted by her old nurse. Meanwhile Odysseus began his journey to the city on foot. In order to protect him from prying eyes, Athene covered him with a mist. Soon he saw the houses and the towers of the Sea Kings. Reaching a little square, he was greeted by Athene in the guise of a maiden carrying a pitcher to fetch water. He asked her where he could find the palace of Alcinous. She said she would show him the way and added:

"Don't talk to anyone, because my people, the proud Sea Kings, are very suspicious towards strangers."

When they got to the palâce, Athene told Odysseus to walk boldly in and go straight up to the Queèn, whose name was Arete.

"She is held in high honour by her husband and her children," Athene said, "and by all other men. She is wise, and if you can gain her goodwill she will help you as no one else can."

Then Athene, still in the form of the maiden with the pitcher, made her departure, and Odysseus entered the palace. The sight caused him to marvel, for the walls shone like the full moon; they were of bronze and the doors plated with gold. The great hall was lined with seats covered with fine cloths which the women of the house had woven. There were fifty maidservants in the palace of Alcinous, to do the cooking, the spinning and the weaving. They were as skilled at their weaving as the Sea Kings were at managing their swift ships. Outside the palace was a rich and beautiful garden, where grew all manner of fruit—pomegranates, grapes, apples and figs—so that they gave a sweet harvest all the year round. There were beds full of bright flowers, and two fountains, one to water the garden and the other for passers-by to drink at.

Dazzled by the beauty of the garden and the splendour of the palace, Odysseus went through the hall to where the King and Queen were seated at one end. The Sea Kings and the princess were sitting round the table with wine cups before them; none saw him because of the cloud of invisibility which Athene had wrapped about him. But when he reached Queen Arete, the cloud dispersed, and everyone marvelled to see the stranger in their midst. Odysseus knelt before the Queen and said:

"Great Queen, take pity on me and help a poor, travel-worn stranger to return to his home and his people. I will pray the gods to send happiness and prosperity to you and all your house."

All were silent, until an old, wise lord said:

"Alcinous, let this stranger be given an honourable place at your table, and let us all drink to his health."

Alcinous led Odysseus by the hand to a place at his side. Servants were commanded to bring water to wash his hands, and food and wine were set before him. When the feast was over, Alcinous told his guests to come to the palace next morning, when they would sit in council and hear the stranger's tale.

"Noble Alcinous," said Odysseus, "I could make a long history of all my griefs and misfortunes, but now all I wish is to return safely to my own country. In the morning, I will beg you to help me on my way."

When the nobles had departed for their houses, Odysseus was left alone with the King and Queen. Now the Queen had been looking closely at the doublet and cloak worn by Odysseus, and she knew that they had been made by herself and her servants.

"Stranger," said Arete, looking into Odysseus' weather-beaten face, "Where do you come from? Who gave you the clothes you are wearing?"

Then Odysseus told the Queen how he had stayed for years on the island of Calypso and how he had made himself a raft and put to sea, for the only thought in his mind was somehow to return to his own country. He told her, how after seventeen days he had been wrecked by the anger of Poseidon and cast up on the coast of the Sea Kings' land. He told how he had passed the night under the bushes, and now next day he had seen Nausicaa and her maidens who had given him food and clothing.

"These are the clothes I am wearing now," he said. "Your daughter told me how to reach your palace, after she herself departed with the wagon and the mules."

"My daughter did well," said Alcinous, "except in one matter. She should have brought you to the palace herself."

"Noble sir," replied Odysseus, "your daughter did right. I had feared that if I had come to your palace in her presence, you might have been offended to see her with a stranger."

"I would not have taken offence," said Alcinous.

"If you should choose to stay here and marry my daughter, it would give me the keenest pleasure. You are the sort of man I look to have for a son-in-law. But we will not try to keep you here if you are set on returning to your own country. Stay with us tonight, and tomorrow one of our fastest ships shall be made ready to carry you wherever you desire to go."

So Odysseus went gladly to rest, for he was weary; and in the morning the King roused him and took him to the public square near the harbour. Here they sat down on the stone seats while a herald went round the town bidding the people come and see the lordly stranger. When the square was thronged with townspeople, Alcinous stood up and said:

"My people, I do not know this stranger's name. But yesterday he came to my house and asked for help to sail back to his own country. Let us treat him as is our custom with strangers in our midst. Let us give him the help he asks. Prepare a swift ship and choose fifty of your most skilful sailors. Then come to the palace where we will hold a feast in honour of our visitor."

After a ship was made ready, the princes crowded into the hall. A minstrel came in, led by a herald, for he was blind. He had lost his eyesight, but he had the voice of a great singer. He sang of the siege of Troy and of the heroes who had died there. The minstrel's singing brought bitter tears to Odysseus' eyes. He hid his face in his cloak; only Alcinous knew that he was weeping.

So he ended the feast and told his guests that they ought to give the stranger an exhibition of their skill at games. They threw quoits, wrestled, boxed and ran races. Then one of the Sea Kings said to the others:

"Let us ask the stranger if he has a particular skill in one or other game. He looks strong and well built."

But when they challenged Odysseus, he shook his head sadly and said:

"I am not in the mood for games. I would rather be left to my sorrow. All I can think of is the wife and the home I left so long ago. All I want from your King and his people is to be helped on my way."

Then one of the young men, whose name was Euryalus, scoffed at Odysseus and said:

"I can well understand why you have no skill in games. I should think you have spent your life as a trader, buying, selling and making bargains. No wonder you will not join in our sports."

Odysseus frowned angrily at the young man and said:

"The gods have given you grace and strength, young man, but they have not given you courtesy. Your rude words have stung me, and I will show you what I can do, stiff and weary though I am with the toils and hardships of my wandering."

So saying, he did not even stop to remove his cloak but stooped and picked up a huge stone quoit. He swung it round and hurled it through the air so that all the onlookers shrank back in fear and amazement. The quoit came to rest far beyond all the others. He smiled as he turned to Euryalus and said:

"There! Make as good a throw as that, young men. Or would you rather I wrestled with you, or boxed, or ran races? I can shoot an arrow too, if that is what you want."

At this there was silence until Alcinous said:

"There is no doubt of your strength and skill, my

friend. We have fast ships but, to tell you the truth, games and sports are not our strong point. We like dancing best, so now let two of my sons give you an exhibition of their ability."

A space was cleared, a minstrel struck up a lively tune on his pipes, and two princes danced with agility and grace, throwing a crimson ball back and forth between them, catching it in the air and dancing all the while, until Odysseus marvelled at their nimbleness.

When the dance was finished, Alcinous told all the Kings to go and fetch gifts for Odysseus to take with him on his journey home.

"Euryalus," he said, "shall make a special gift, to pay for his rudeness."

The young man readily agreed and presented Odysseus with a handsome bronze sword with a cunningly-wrought scabbard of carved ivory. He smiled at Odysseus in a frank and friendly way and said:

"Pardon me, sir, for my rough words. I beg you, let them be forgotten; and may I wish you a safe and speedy return to your home from which you have been so long away."

Slinging the sword over his shoulder, Odysseus said:

"I thank you for your kindness, friend. May good fortune go with you always, and may you never stand in need of this fine blade!"

Then Alcinous led Odysseus back into the palace where the princes were already drinking wine. Before entering the hall, Odysseus went to the room that had been set aside for him and bathed. As he entered the hall, he saw that the Princess Nausicaa was standing at the door in all her beauty.

"I have come to say farewell, stranger," she said in a low voice. "When you are home again, think of me, for I was the first to help you when you were cast up on this shore."

"I will never forget you, Princess," answered Odysseus. "You will always be to me like one of the gods, for it was you who brought me back to life after my desperate journey."

Odysseus went and took his seat beside Alcinous, and the minstrel played and sang a song of Troy. Once more Odysseus wept, so that the King told the minstrel to cease singing. He turned to his guest.

"Now, stranger, surely your secret is out. If the tale of Troy causes you such grief, tell us whether you lost a friend or a kinsman in that war. Or what is it that makes you weep?"

So Odysseus told the King and his guests that he was Odysseus. That, from the time of the burning of Troy, he had been away from his home and his people for a full ten years, and that he longed to return. The Princes listened with close attention and wonder as their guest kept them from their beds, telling of all his adventures on the storm-tossed seas—how he had blinded the Cyclops Polyphemus and passed the island of the Sirens, how he had come safely through the straits between Scylla and Charybdis, and how he had lost his ship and all his men and been wrecked on the island of Calypso. He told of his visit to the enchantress Circe; and finally he described his escape from Calypso's island on his raft, and how it was broken to pieces, and of his being thrown up on the Sea Kings' shore when he was almost drowned beneath the waves.

When Odysseus' tale was done, the guests all departed for their homes. In the morning they returned with their gifts, and Alcinous sacrificed an ox to Zeus to ensure a safe journey for Odysseus. All day they feasted and drank, and all the time Odysseus looked towards the sun, longing for it to go down beyond the western wave. That was to be the time for his departure. At last Odysseus turned to King Alcinous and Queen Arete and bade them farewell. He thanked them for all their kindness and their entertainment, and wished them good fortune, happiness and long life.

The heralds led the way to the ship moored in the harbour. The Queen sent her servants with warm clothing for the voyage; the rowers took their places on the benches, while Odysseus lay down and stretched himself out in the stern. As the ship left, a deep, sweet sleep fell upon Odysseus. Once out of the harbour, the sailors hoisted sail and the ship sped as fast as a hawk through the dark waters. All through the night the hero who had suffered so much and been buffeted by so many storms slept peacefully and forgot his sorrows.

When the morning star arose, the ship came in sight of Ithaca. Here there was a haven so calm that ships might ride in it without anchor. At the end of the harbour was a great olive tree and a cave where sea-nymphs wove their blue garments and mixed their wine. Inside the cave were two springs of clear water. Into this harbour, well known to the Sea Kings, the ship was rowed. The sailors beached the vessel and lifted the still sleeping Odysseus out of the stern. They wrapped him in rugs and laid him gently on the sand. Lastly, they lifted out of the ship all the gifts they had given him and piled them carefully against the gnarled trunk of the olive tree so that he should find them when he woke. Then they dragged the ship into the water, climbed aboard and silently rowed away.

11

Odysseus in Ithaca

WHEN ODYSSEUS AWOKE, he had no idea that he was at last in his own country. For one thing, he had not set foot on it for twenty years. In addition, Athene had spread about him a sea mist so that he could see only a few yards around him. In this she was, as ever, thoughtful. If he had been seen and perhaps recognised by anyone on the island, word would have reached the suitors, and his life would have been in mortal danger. So Odysseus rose to his feet, groaning and striking his breast.

"What is this country," he asked, "and who are its people? Are they savages or friendly men? Why have I been landed and left here, deserted, with the treasures of the Sea Kings? Why could I not have been brought to some friendly people who might have taken me in safety to my own land?"

"Ah, woe is me," he went on, groaning in his misery, "the Sea Kings are not men of their word. They promised to take me to my own country, and instead they have abandoned me on a strange and desolate coast. How am I to look after myself here, and guard my treasures in safety?"

Next Odysseus went to the heap of gifts and counted through them carefully—the garments, the precious

vessels and the weapons. He found that there was
nothing missing. At least he had not been robbed.

Then Odysseus heard a light step approaching down
the footpath that led down to the shore. He gripped
his sword more firmly for fear the stranger should be
hostile. But he saw that the man who approached was
a young shepherd of gentle appearance. There were
sandals on his feet and a javelin in his hand. Over his
shoulders he wore a neatly folded cloak. It was
Odysseus' protectress, Athene, in disguise.

"Friend," said Odysseus, lowering his sword. "I am
a stranger in this land, and you are the first of its
inhabitants I have encountered. These things you see
are all my wordly possessions. Will you be a friend to
me and help me to defend them? What country is this,
and who are its people?"

Athene smiled and said:

"My friend, either you must be very simple-minded
or you must have come from a great way off. This is a
steep and rocky island, suitable only for the raising of
goats and swine, but not for horses. But there is
plenty of water, so that the land is fruitful. On its
slopes grow olives, grapes and even corn. This is, in
short, an island called Ithaca, whose name is famous.
It has been heard of from the islands of the east to the
farthest west. Yes," added Athene, smiling a little as if
to herself, "it has even been heard of on the windy
plains of Troy."

When he heard the name of Ithaca, Odysseus' heart
gave a great leap inside him. He could have fainted
for joy, but he felt he must not give himself away
before the strange young shepherd. In fact, so natural
was it with Odysseus to be cunning and hide the truth
for fear of imprudence, that he told Athene a story

only partly true. He did not wish to give away all his secret until he knew he was safe. He had always feared betrayal.

"I myself was at Troy," he said, "and after the war I made my way back to my home in Crete."

He then told a cock-and-bull story of how he had been outlawed from Crete on account of a murder he had committed, and bribed a crew of Phoenician sailors to take him to Greece. But they had been blown off their course and had landed him and his treasures on the strange shore where he now found himself.

How Athene, who knew the whole truth, must have laughed inwardly as she heard this nonsense, but at the same time she applauded him for his caution and his inventiveness. Gently she stretched out her hand and touched Odysseus on the sleeve. He saw that it was the hand of a woman, and, looking into her face, he recognised his friend and protectress, Athene.

"Oh what a master deceiver you are, my Odysseus!" she said. "But I too am known among the gods for my cunning. It is time for us to be honest with each other. I have been your friend and companion through all your trials. It was I who made the Sea Kings carry you to your own country and put you ashore with your store of treasures."

"It is now my duty," the goddess went on, "to tell you of the troubles and trials which still await you. It is necessary that, for the time being, you remain unknown to the people of Ithaca, even to your own dear kith and kin. You must above all be patient, as you have been patient during all your years of hardship and peril."

"The goddess Athene," replied Odysseus, "disguises herself in many forms. You were with me, I know, at

Troy, but since then I have never been allowed to see you face to face. I can believe that you have always been my protectress. But speak to me honestly, I beg you, now that I see you directly. Am I indeed in my own country, or is it to mock me that you tell me I am at last in my native Ithaca? Tell me the whole truth, I beseech you."

"You are right to ask that question," replied the goddess. "It is true that since you were at Troy I have never been able to reveal myself to you in my true form, for fear of angering my uncle Poseidon, your mortal enemy. But now that you are safe from his vengeance, standing in your own country, let me show it to you so that you will believe me and never again doubt my word."

So saying, Athene rolled away the sea mist and said:

"There is the harbour that you once knew so well. There is the great olive tree at the end of it, and the cave of the nymphs. You cannot have forgotten these."

Then Odysseus gazed about him and marvelled at the sight of the scenes he had once known so well. When at last he was sure that he was indeed standing in his own land, he knelt down and kissed the earth. Next he made a vow to the nymphs and swore that, if Athene allowed him to return to his own house and see once again his wife and son, he would make a solemn sacrifice in their honour.

Athene then told Odysseus that the first thing to do was to hide his treasures so as not to attract the attention of passers by, who might be tempted to steal them. So with her help he carried into the cave his gifts of gold, bronze and silver and his rich garments and piled them up. Then Athene rolled a stone over the mouth of the cave to cover it over.

Next the goddess and the wanderer sat down together under the great olive tree, and she told him about the suitors who had invaded his home and were plotting to carry off Penelope. She pointed out the danger in which Odysseus stood, adding:

"Son of Laertes, these are ruthless and desperate men, who will stop at nothing to get what they want. We must consider how best to overcome them."

Odysseus stroked his beard thoughtfully.

"Goddess," he said at length, "I am indeed in mortal danger. How fortunate that you did not let me at once hurry home and fall into their hands. As you say, let us think what to do. All I will say now is that, as long as you are at my side to help me, I care not if there are three hundred of them."

"It is not so bad as that, my son," said Athene with a laugh, "but I promise to be always at your side. Meanwhile, the first thing I must do is to alter your form so that no one will recognise you."

She moved close to Odysseus and laid her hands on his face, his arms and his shoulders. So great was the power of the goddess that at once his skin lost its smoothness and its healthy bronze colour and became old, yellow and wrinkled. His golden hair, hanging luxuriantly about his neck, became grey and straggling, and much of it fell out. His fine mantle was replaced by a foul tunic, coarse and patched, stained and torn with much wear. His eyes became bleared and gummy, so as to make him unwelcome in the sight, not only of the suitors, but even of his wife and son.

"Now," said Athene, looking with pleasure at the bent figure of the disreputable old beggar, "you must first find out the swine-herd Eumaeus and go to him. He it is who looks after the swine belonging to your house, and he is loyal to your son and to your faithful Penelope. You will find him with the swine at the rock of Corax. They feed well there on roots, acorns, and have fresh water to drink from the spring which gushes out beneath the rock. You must stay with Eumaeus while I go off to bring back Telemachus from his voyage to Sparta. There he is the guest of Menelaus and the gracious Helen, while here in Ithaca the suitors await his return in order to do him harm. But have no fear. I will protect him."

With these words Athene bade Odysseus farewell and set off on her winged sandals for Sparta. Odysseus, in the guise of the foul old beggar, was left to find the swine-herd.

12

Eumaeus the swine-herd

ODYSSEUS TURNED HIS back on the sea and took
the track that led him inland. It climbed steadily
until, becoming steeper, it led him among the
hills and groves. Here, following the directions given
to him by the goddess, he came to a low, simple
house surrounded by a wall. While his master had been
away, Eumaeus the swine-herd had built it for himself.
He had surrounded the wall with a fence of oak and
thorn, so that no thief or enemy could break in. In
the courtyard he had constructed twelve sties, each big
enough to hold fifty sows. The male swine, the boars,
slept outside the sties. There were far fewer of the
boars than of the sows, because the suitors had had
them slain for their feasts. The sties were not full, so
that the total number of the swine was no more than
about three hundred and sixty. They were guarded by
four fierce dogs.

Eumaeus had four younger swine-herds to help him.
At the time of Odysseus' arrival, one of them was away,
taking a boar to the palace for the feast of the suitors;
the other three were in the hills with the animals.
Eumaeus, alone in his dwelling, was fashioning leather
sandals from oxhide. As soon as they heard Odysseus,
the hounds rushed towards him, baying. At once
Odysseus sat down on the ground and dropped his

H

beggar's staff. Eumaeus threw aside the sandal on which he was working, ran from the house and called off the dogs. Pale and shaking, he spoke to the beggar at his gate.

Odysseus got up from the ground, helping himself to his feet with his staff.

"Stranger," said Eumaeus, "you nearly lost your life at my gate. This would have added yet one more grief to the many which the gods have sent me. Here I live by myself, fattening up my master's beasts for others to devour, while he, no doubt, is hungering on a distant shore—if, that is to say, he is still alive."

Inside the cottage the swine-herd spread brushwood on the floor and laid a hide upon it, bidding his guest be seated. Odysseus was humbly grateful for the courtesy of his reception. He called down upon the swine-herd the blessing of Zeus.

"That is the least I can do," said Eumaeus. "In the old days would my master ever have turned away the humblest beggar from his door? Is it not well known that strangers are under the protection of almighty Zeus?"

The swine-herd heaved a deep sigh and added:

"You are welcome to my humble house. If my master had been here, he would have given me a little land for myself, on which I could spend the latter years of my life. But alas, I fear he has long been dead."

With these words Eumaeus went out and brought in two young swine, which he killed and dressed with wine and barley flour. He cut the flesh in pieces and roasted it on the fire. Then he poured more wine into a bowl of ivy wood and bade Odysseus drink. When the meat was roasted, the swine-herd said:

"This is the best I can offer you, stranger. These are mere sucking pigs. All the best and fattest are kept for the feasts of those who swarm about my mistress's house."

"Tell me of these men," said Odysseus.

"You must know, stranger," Eumaeus said, "that my master was a great and rich prince. When he went away to the war in Troy twenty years ago, he left his wife to manage his household. All went well until his return was despaired of. A crowd of princes and lords from Ithaca and the neighbouring islands came swarming about the palace. They told my mistress that her husband would never come back and that she had better marry one of them. She has always refused, believing in her heart that her own lord will return. Meanwhile, they take advantage of the laws of hospitality and feed on my master's swine—yes, and his goats and his wine as well. Every day they riot and feast in his courtyard; every day they waste more and more of our substance. No one can see an end of the waste and disorder."

"Tell me, friend," Odysseus said when he had feasted himself to the full on the roast meat and wine, "who was this rich lord, your master? Perhaps in my wanderings I have heard news of him."

Eumaeus said with a bitter sneer:

"Many wanderers have come this way with tales of my master. But they are false—all false. These wandering liars are always sent to tell their stories to my mistress, because she loves to listen to them and always gives them a hospitable welcome. No doubt you, too, my beggar friend, would make up a tale for my mistress's ear in exchange for a new doublet and cloak. But I know better. My master is dead, I tell you, and his body was long ago the prey to dogs and carrion birds. Or perhaps he is drowned and his bones have been picked clean, by the fish. Now they lie whitening on some sandy shore. My master is dead, and all those who loved him are sorrowing for his memory. No one grieves for him more piteously than I, for he was the kindest master in the world. His name was Odysseus."

Odysseus looked long and searchingly into the swine-herd's troubled eyes. Then he laid a gnarled hand on his sturdy shoulder and said solemnly:

"My friend, you have received me with generosity, and I cannot abuse your generosity by lying to you. I swear to you by Zeus that Odysseus lives, and that he will return to his former home. Then, and not before, I will claim the reward of bringing good tidings—the new doublet and cloak of which you spoke. Heaven knows", he went on, looking ruefully down at his tattered rags, "I need them now. But I will not ask for them until they are my due. I promise you that, before a year is out, you shall look upon your old master once more."

Eumaeus refused to be comforted.

"I cannot believe you," he said, "and if you claim the reward of a bearer of good tidings, it will not be I who gives it to you. Let us talk of other things. Odysseus left behind him a son, Telemachus, now a fine, well-grown young man of twenty. He is not the equal of his father for strength and beauty. Nevertheless, he is the hope of his father's house. Some evil influence has lately fallen upon him. He has lost his wits and gone off on a foolish expedition to far Pylos to seek tidings of his father. Now these suitors of whom I told you lie in wait for him to destroy him on his return. For, as the only son of Odysseus, he may stand in the way of their getting the kingdom for themselves.

"But now, stranger," said Eumaeus, "tell me about yourself. Who are your parents, of what country do you come, and by what ship did you find your way here?"

Now Odysseus did not want to reveal himself to the swine-herd before it suited him. He feared that, if it were known that Odysseus himself had returned, he would be in mortal danger. Everything would be told in the gods' good time. So he told a long story, partly true and partly imaginary, of how he was a native of Crete.

"When my father died," he said, "I was left some money and goods, so that I did not need to work on the land. With the help of the goddess Athene I gained a reputation for being a mighty fighter. I went off to fight in many lands, and with the booty I won I became rich. In the end I joined the expedition of Agamemnon, king of the Greeks, and sailed against Troy. We fought for nine long years, and in the tenth year we destroyed the city with fire and with out bronze weapons. We returned to our ships and sailed back to Greece. But the gods sent wind and storms, and we were scattered and separated from each other.

"I returned to my home in Crete, but before a month was out I became restless. How could a man who had seen such action and adventure as I settle down to the humdrum life of a farmer? I joined an expedition to Egypt. But there my men rebelled against me and made war on the Egyptians. Many of my followers were killed, and I was taken prisoner. For seven whole years I remained with the King of the

Egyptians, who treated me with honour and gave me many gifts. Then in the eighth year I was persuaded by a false Phoenician trader to sail with him to his own country. He made me promises of great riches. So we went aboard his ship, and I learned that his real intention was to sell me at a high price in Libya, along the African coast. However, a storm blew up, the ship was wrecked, and all the company drowned. I succeeded in clinging to a broken mast. For nine whole days I was tossed and buffeted on the waves until I was cast up half dead on an island. Here the king took pity on me, clothed and fed me. On this island I had news of Odysseus. The king told me that, shortly before that, he had entertained Odysseus and sent him on his way back to his own country. I did not myself see Odysseus, but I saw the gifts which he had left behind. In a few days I embarked on a ship where my ill luck was still not at an end. For the sailors stripped me of my good clothing and gave me these rags which now you see. They left me on the shore, whence I made my way to your hospitable house. It must be that the gods were on my side, and to them I give thanks for my salvation.''

Eumaeus had listened to Odysseus with the greatest interest and sympathy, but he shook his head, still refusing to believe that part of the tale which concerned his master.

"Be that as it may,'' Odysseus said, "but I swear it is true. If I am proved right, then you must give me a cloak and a doublet and send me away. If I am proved wrong, then let your men take me to a high cliff and throw me over. In this way I shall be an example to all who may come and deceive you with false tales.''

Eumaeus once more shook his head vigorously and smote the table with his fist.

"No," he said, "I will never agree to such a bargain. How could I treat in this way a man who has enjoyed my hospitality?"

The sound of the men's voices, mixed with the grunting and squealing of animals, was heard in the distance. Eumaeus went on:

"But now I hear my men coming back from the woods. They will be with us in a minute. Let us get supper ready for all of us."

The sound of slithering hooves and grunting swine was heard immediately outside the cottage, as the men drove their charges into the sties. Eumaeus went outside and told one of the herdsmen to kill the best of the boars in honour of their guest.

"Here is one beast those human beasts shan't get," he said.

Logs were split to make a fire. Eumaeus was always mindful of his duty to the gods who send us all things. First he cut bristles from the boar's head and threw them on to the fire, where they singed and crackled, giving off a bitter, pungent smell. Then, as soon as the animal was cut up, he took the fattest portion and made a burnt offering of it to the gods. When all was ready, the next finest portion was given to Odysseus, and everyone feasted and drank. After the meal, the four herdsmen went to get their rest. They slept on the floor of the cottage, and a bed was made there for Odysseus also. He was given fleecy coverings in case the night should turn cold. Eumaeus bade his guest good-night and said that he would go and sleep outside, for his first thought was always for the safety of the swine. This delighted the heart of

Odysseus, for he saw that his servant was still faithful to him, even though he believed his master dead. Eumaeus took his sword and a heap of coverings and went out to sleep in an opening in the rock within earshot of the boars.

13
Telemachus meets his father

ALL THIS WHILE Telemachus was the guest of Menelaus and Helen in the fertile land of Sparta. To him journeyed the swift-footed Athene, to bid him to be on his way home. She found him on his bed in the porch of the King's palace. He had spent a restless night, thinking about his father and wondering if he would ever see him again.

"Telemachus," said the goddess, "you should make haste to get back to Ithaca. You linger here too long. You have left evil men behind you, and they lie in wait to do you mischief. Your mother is hard pressed. They are trying to persuade her to forget your father and marry Eurymachus. Your grandfather Laertes and your mother's kin are also trying to persuade her to choose this man, for he offers more splendid gifts than any of the others. If she hearkens to the charms and persuasions of Eurymachus, she may at length forget your father. Make haste, or you may be robbed of all you have. But as you sail home, be on your guard, for your enemies lie in wait for you in the narrow seas between Ithaca and Samos. Here they will try to wreck your ship and bring about your destruction. Do not steer near the land, and sail by night as well as by day. One of the gods who loves you will send you a fair wind to carry you to safety.

Now listen to me carefully. When you reach the harbour, let neither you nor your men go to the city. But go alone to the house of Eumaeus the swine-herd. Have you understood all this?"

Telemachus, who was by now fully awake, assured the goddess that he had taken in all she had said. Then she bade him farewell and sped off on winged sandals to Mount Olympus, home of the deathless gods. As soon as it was day and the palace was fully awake, Telemachus sought Menelaus and said:

"O son of Atreus, send me home today, I beg, for I long to see once more the shores of Ithaca."

Menelaus answered:

"If you long to see your home once more, I will not keep you here. But first, let me give you a parting present."

He went to his treasure house and brought out a cup and a bowl of finely-wrought silver, and Helen brought him a robe made by herself. It shone pale and glowing, like the light of stars.

"Take this, dear Telemachus, in memory of Helen. Keep it safe and give it to your bride upon her marriage day. May joy go with you."

Then Telemachus and Pisistratus, the son of Nestor who had come with him on his journey from Pylos, yoked the horses to the chariot. When they had bidden farewell to Menelaus and Helen, they drove out of the courtyard.

Menelaus bade farewell to the young men and told Pisistratus to greet Nestor for him.

"He was my friend", he said, "when we fought together at Troy, and I always think kindly of him."

Then Telemachus looked solemn as he thought of his own father.

"If only I might find Odysseus in Ithaca when I
return. Then what joy it will give me to tell him of
all your kindness to me."

As Telemachus spoke, a shadow crossed the sun,
and an eagle flew overhead with a tame goose in his
claws. Pisistratus said:

"That is surely a sign sent by the high gods.
Tell us what it means, Menelaus."

Menelaus paused, not knowing what to say. It was
Helen who interpreted the omen.

"That eagle swooped down from its nest in the
high mountains and seized the goose from our palace.
In the same way Odysseus will swoop down and
revenge himself upon the suitors."

Thus heartened, Telemachus and the son of Nestor
drove away across the level plain, until the sun went
down and darkness fell upon the dusty road. Next day
they reached Pylos, where the ship lay waiting in the
harbour. Telemachus bade farewell to his young friend
and said that he would for ever remember him with
gratitude.

"Just as your father Nestor was friends with my
father," said Telemachus, "so let us too be friends."

Just as Telemachus was about to go on board, a
man named Theoclymenus, who had the gift of
second sight, hurried up and begged to travel with
him. He said he was fleeing from his own country
where he had had the ill fortune to kill a man.
Telemachus took him on board. Athene sent a fresh
breeze, and the ship bounded over the waves.
Telemachus remembered her words to him in Sparta
and was careful not to sail near the coast of Samos.
In this way he escaped the suitors. When they
neared the shore, Telemachus said to the stranger:

"In the old days I would have asked you as guest to my own house, but now you would get an ill welcome. My mother keeps herself apart in her own room; my father is away, and Eurymachus is in charge. He is no friend to strangers."

Then he told the crew that he desired to land before the city was reached, and ordered one of his men to entertain Theoclymenus while he himself was away. The ship was beached, and Telemachus left the men in charge. He took a path leading inland and made for the house of Eumaeus the swine-herd.

When Telemachus arrived, he found Odysseus and the swine-herd getting breakfast ready. The dogs knew Telemachus and greeted him affectionately, wagging their tails and jumping up for caresses from his hand. Odysseus remarked to Eumaeus:

"A friend of yours has come. The dogs welcome him."

Hardly had he spoken when his own son stood at the open doorway. Eumaeus was so taken aback by the sudden appearance of Telemachus that he started up and dropped the bowl in which he was mixing wine. Great was his joy and relief at seeing his young master's safe return. He fell on the young man's neck and kissed him as a father might kiss an only child.

"Dear boy," said Eumaeus, "so you have come home at last. When you began your journey to Pylos, I was afraid I might never see you again. Come in and let me look at you. You are not a frequent visitor nowadays, for you are kept in the town watching that mob of greedy men."

"As you wish, good Eumaeus," Telemachus answered. "I have come especially to see you and to hear news of my mother. How is she?"

"She has not changed," the swine-herd said. "She spends her time weeping and waiting for the return of Odysseus."

As Telemachus entered the room, Odysseus got up and offered him his seat.

"No," said Telemachus, "keep your seat, stranger. The swine-herd will make up another for me." So a seat was placed for Telemachus beside the one Odysseus sat on, and food was prepared for him. When the feasting was done, Telemachus asked who the old beggarly man was and how he had come to Ithaca. Eumaeus told the young man the story which Odysseus had told him and begged him to give the stranger his protection.

But Telemachus shook his head.

"I cannot take him to the palace," he said. "That is no place of hospitality. The suitors would make fun of him and ill treat him. I will give him a new cloak and doublet and a sharp sword and send him on his way."

"Young sir," Odysseus said respectfully, "may I be allowed to speak? From what this man has told me, it seems that great wrong has been done to you in your house, and is being done every day. Are you hated by your own people? Can you get no support from your brothers? Ah, if I were as young as you, or as strong as your father Odysseus, or if I were Odysseus himself, I would go to your palace and attack the suitors single-handed. Rather than see shame and disgrace done in your house, I would die in combat."

Telemachus replied:

"Listen to me, stranger. My kinsfolk do not hate me, but I have no brothers to give me aid. All-powerful Zeus has made me the only child of my parents. My

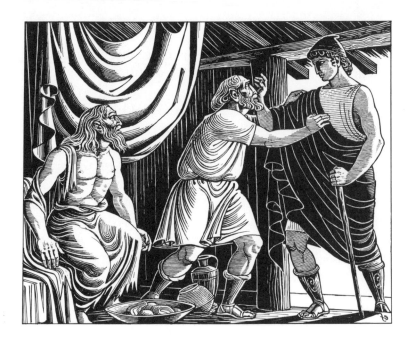

house is full of enemies, who make love to my mother and threaten my safety. I am at my wits' end, not knowing how the matter will turn out."

Then Telemachus said to the swine-herd:

"Go at once to the house, Eumaeus, and tell my mother that I have come back safely. I will wait here till you return."

"I will do as you say, master," replied Eumaeus, "but shall I not go first to your grandfather Laertes and take the news to him? It will give him fresh life. Since you went away, he has done nothing but sit and stare into the hearth. He eats nothing and pines away in bitter grief, thinking you will never return."

But Telemachus would not hear of this. He told Eumaeus to go directly to the Queen and tell her to send word to Laertes by one of her servants.

So the swine-herd strode from the house and made his way towards the palace. Immediately Athene, tall and graceful, appeared in the doorway and revealed herself to Odysseus. The dogs saw her and were afraid. They whined and slunk away to the corners of the yard. Telemachus could not see the goddess.

At a sign from Athene, Odysseus came out to her beside the doorway and she said to him in low tones:

"Odysseus. Now is the moment to show yourself to your son. Tell him everything. Then arm yourselves and go out together to do battle with the suitors. I shall be near you in the fight. My love and protection will never leave you."

Then the goddess touched the old beggar and restored him to his former beauty and splendour. His scraggy, grey beard became thick and golden, his hair long and plentiful. The bleary roughness of his skin gave way to the smoothness of polished bronze. His eyes became bright and alert. When Odysseus went back into the swine-herd's house, Telemachus marvelled at the strength and beauty of the man and turned away his eyes, for he thought he was looking at a god. At last Telemachus spoke, shyly and with hesitation:

"Stranger," he said, "if indeed you are the man who went out of this room a few minutes ago, you have changed utterly. If you were a god in disguise and have now regained your proper form, let us make sacrifices to you in due order."

Odysseus stepped up to the young man and laid a hand on his shoulder.

"Telemachus," he said resolutely, 'I am no god. I am your own dear father. For my sake you have put up with bitter wrongs and the scorn of evil men.

Then he solemnly kissed his son, and both of them wept. But Telemachus could not believe him. Since he had been an infant in arms, he had never seen his father. How could this godlike creature be the man for whom he and his mother had been waiting and praying all these long years?

"You are not my father," he said quietly but firmly. "You are a god sent here to deceive me. Perhaps you have come to betray me into the power of my mother's enemies. No mortal man could do as you have done in the last few minutes. Just now you were an old, ragged man, tottering and infirm; now, within a few minutes, you are strong, godlike and upstanding. This change is beyond mortal power."

"I am the only Odysseus who will ever return to you," answered the other. "Athene, who has always been the friend and protector of me and my house, has brought about this change. She can do what she will with mortal men. She can make a man young or old in an instant, strong or feeble, rich or poor. Such power have the immortal gods."

So Telemachus at last believed and fell upon his father's shoulders and wept. They wept together and would have continued like this until evening, had not the young man wiped away his tears and asked Odysseus how he came to Ithaca. Odysseus told him the true story of how the Sea Kings had brought him to Ithaca and how Athene had befriended him and sent him up to the swine-herd's house.

"But now tell me about these suitors," said Odysseus. "How many are there and what chance have we two against them? Are they strong and well armed?"

"Father," Telemachus answered, "I well know your fame as a hero and a warrior. I have been told stories of it all my life. But how could even you, with only one other to help, match a host of a hundred and eight men. They are the best warriors of Ithaca and the neighbouring islands. We have no hope unless you can think of some champion who would bring a force of fighting men to help us."

"But my son," said Odysseus, "what if Zeus himself and Athene are fighting at our side? Would we then need others to help us?"

"They are the best of champions," Telemachus agreed.

"When the fighting begins," his father said, "they will be with us. You may be sure of that. Now listen carefully to my plan. When morning comes, you must return to the palace as if nothing had happened and mix with the suitors. Eumaeus will bring me to the town disguised once more as the old beggar. I shall go to the palace, and if the suitors ill-use me, or perhaps hit me, or drive me from the house, you must bear it all. You must forget that I am a guest and need your protection; you must even forget that I am your true father. You may reproach them if you like, but they will take no notice; the day of their fate is near, and no doubt their insolence grows. Above all, my son, tell no one that Odysseus has returned—neither Laertes nor the swine-herd, nor even your mother Penelope. We must keep that a secret until we are sure who are our friends."

Telemachus said he had understood everything, and his father could trust him. He would tell no one the secret.

Meanwhile Eumaeus had gone to the palace with the news of Telemachus' return. This was bad tidings for the suitors, for now they knew that their plot against the young man's life had failed. They sat outside looking down at the harbour, and as they did so, their ship returned. The suitors went to the public square to greet their companions. With them they discussed what they should do. It was agreed that, as soon as an opportunity showed itself, they would murder Telemachus. When this was decided, they returned to the palace and sprawled about the hall and the courtyard.

Now Medon, who was herald in Odysseus' household, had heard all the suitors had said, so he went secretly to his mistress Penelope and told her. As soon as Penelope understood that the suitors plotted to kill her son, she put on a brightly-coloured shawl and went downstairs with her maidens. She stood at the entrance to the hall. She looked round and singled out Antinous.

"Evil and insolent Antinous," she said in a voice of terrible accusation, so trembling with anger that everyone stopped his mouth and listened to her. "How can it be that in Ithaca you are counted one of their wisest men? No, you are acting with criminal folly, plotting to kill my son. He is helpless before you, but Zeus is the friend to our house and the protector of the innocent. He will avenge our wrongs, and a terrible doom will pursue you. Not only are you defying the gods, Antinous, you are guilty of base ingratitude. Have you not heard how Odysseus once shielded and helped your father? Is this not the man whose substance you now waste and whose son you are plotting to murder?"

Antinous said nothing, but the smooth-tonged Eurymachus spoke soft words.

"No one, honoured Queen," he said, "shall hurt a hair of your son's head while I am alive. He is a noble youth and I revere him."

Penelope could say no more, for the words of Eurymachus were fair. But there was deceit in his heart, as he plotted to put Telemachus to death.

That evening Eumaeus returned to his house and found Odysseus, once more in the guise of the ragged beggar man, preparing supper with the help of Telemachus.

"What news of the suitors?" Telemachus asked. "Have they got back home, or do they still wait in the narrow seas by Samos to take me prisoner?"

"I don't know, master," answered the swine-herd. "I did not stay in town to hear the news. But one thing I saw. That was the entrance of a fast ship into the harbour. On its deck were armed men. These may have been some of the suitors, but I cannot be sure."

Telemachus exchanged a knowing smile with his father, but he was careful that Eumaeus did not see. It would not do for the swine-herd to know there was an understanding between his young master and the old beggarly stranger.

14

Odysseus goes to the palace

NEXT MORNING TELEMACHUS rose with the dawn. He bound on his sandals and took up his heavy spear. He told Eumaeus that he was going to the city to greet his mother.

"As for your guest," he said to Eumaeus, "bring him to the city after me and show him where he may best station himself to beg for food and water. It is no use his staying here in the country. It will be best for him to be in the town where he can earn a living."

"Yes, indeed," agreed Odysseus, still in his beggar's rags. "If I go into the city, there will be strangers there who will be glad to show charity to a needy wanderer. But my rags are a poor covering, so I beg you, dear Eumaeus, to let me stay here until the sun is fully risen and the frosts of dawn melted away."

So Telemachus bade him farewell and set out to sow the seeds of evil for the suitors. When he got to the palace, the first to set eyes on him was the old nurse Eurycleia. She was busy in the hall, spreading skins upon the benches. She and her women gathered about him and showed their pleasure at his safe return. Next Penelope came down from her chamber and embraced him with tears in her eyes.

"Ah, my dear son," said Penelope, "when I learned

that you had left home to journey afar, I was sure I should never see you again. Then I should indeed have been overwhelmed with sorrow. Well now, tell me, what news did you get of your father?"

Telemachus did not answer her directly, but spoke with a new, quiet authority.

"Mother," he said, "the day of vengeance is at hand. Go, you and your maidens, bathe yourselves and put on fresh garments. Prepare to make a solemn sacrifice to the gods, so that they may be our constant help. I myself will go down to the market-place to meet a friend of mine who claims to have seen Odysseus on his wanderings."

Then Telemachus grasped his spear and strode out across the courtyard. He looked so radiant and manly that everyone was impressed, and even the suitors wished him God-speed with respectful words and gestures. Then they huddled together in corners and murmured against him. Before going into the city, Telemachus, avoiding the main body of the suitors, seated himself in a corner of the courtyard near the gate, beckoning to Mentor and two others to join him. These others were Antiphus and Halitherses. These three men had all been friends of his father in the old days. Then Piraeus, captain of the ship on which Telemachus had sailed to Sparta, brought Theoclymenus to see him. This was the man who said that he had had sight of Odysseus on the island of Calypso.

When Telemachus had feasted, his mother drew him aside and reminded him that she had asked him if he had heard any news of Odysseus. Telemachus recounted to his mother how he had journeyed first to Pylos, where Nestor had had no news to give him

about his father, but had sent him on to Sparta. Here
he had been generously entertained by Menelaus and
Helen. Menelaus had had no direct news but was sure
in his mind that Odysseus was alive and would one
day return to Ithaca to be revenged on the suitors.
Penelope was overjoyed at this hopeful news. Then
Theoclymenus, the stranger whom Telemachus had
befriended, came up and repeated what he had said
before—that Odysseus had been seen on the island of
Calypso and that he would assuredly return.

All this while the suitors had been laughing and
roistering in the courtyard and about the palace,
engaging in contests with weight-putting, throwing the
javelin and casting the discus. At last they began to
weary of these pastimes and told their servants to
prepare the usual banquet.

Meanwhile Eumaeus said to Odysseus who was still
in the guise of a ragged beggar:

"It is time, stranger, to be making for the town."

Odysseus agreed, but first begged Eumaeus to give
him a stout staff to help him on his way and to
beat off any dog which might attack him. Eumaeus
did as he was asked, and Odysseus also obtained from
him a shabby old bag with a cord to hang it over his
shoulder. In this he would put all the scraps of food
he could beg.

On their way to the town Odysseus and the swine-
herd had to pass by an alder grove with a spring
sacred to the nymphs. Here they encountered a goat-
herd named Melanthius. With him were two other
herdsmen. They were driving in front of them the
fattest goats of all the herd, to be slain for the feast.

Melanthius addressed Eumaeus in rude, coarse
terms.

"What how, Eumaeus," he said. "Why are you leading that filthy beggar? You are encouraging him to beg his greedy way about the town, sponging on any poor fool with a soft heart. He will find his way up to the palace, I tell you. If he does, he'll get stools thrown at his head. You'd do better to give him to me, swine-herd, so that I can train him up to look after my goats. Then he'll be doing a useful stroke of work for a change."

As he passed the ragged stranger, Melanthius gave him a vicious kick on the hip. Odysseus did not waver but stood firm. Anger rose in his breast, and he was tempted to knock Melanthius to the ground with one blow of his cudgel. This he could easily have done, but he restrained himself. The moment for revenge had not yet come. So he took the goat-herd's blow without protesting.

"Well," said Melanthius, "I must be on my way. One day I shall sell your beggar man into slavery for a good price. Meanwhile I hope the princes at the palace will make short work of that upstart, your master Telemachus. He has no hope, for the day of Odysseus' homecoming is long past. We shall never see him again on this island."

Odysseus himself looked searchingly at Melanthius with his bleary, red-rimmed eyes. The ghost of a mocking smile passed across his face, but he said nothing. Melanthius called to his herdsmen, who were watering the goats at the spring, and went on with them to the palace. Here he sat himself beside Eurymachus who was his protector. He was given meat and wine and wheaten bread.

Slowly Odysseus and the swine-herd followed after Melanthius, and in time they reached the palace. A sound of distant revelry came to Odysseus' ears. He could hear the notes of the lyre and the high-pitched voice of the minstrel Phemius intoning some ballad.

"Ah," he said cunningly, "we must be nearing the home of Odysseus."

"Before we go in," said Eumaeus, "let us decide what to do; either I will go in first and find out if the revellers are in a friendly mood, or you may go first and risk the insults that may greet you. Some of these men do not treat beggars with the generosity that is their due."

Odysseus said it would be best if Eumaeus went on ahead, so he waited outside the yard while the swineherd went in. Then a dog just inside the yard raised its feeble voice. This was Argos, an old hound which had belonged to Odysseus as a mere puppy twenty years before. Since the departure of its master, it had been utterly neglected and now lay on a dung heap plagued by flies and covered with sores. Argos was now so feeble that he was very near death. Something had kept him alive during the years of his old age. Now that he heard strangers at the gate, he stiffened his ears and strained to recognise them. As he made out the voice of Odysseus, the old master who had trained him for the hunt, he dropped his ears, moved his tail feebly and endeavoured to rise to his feet. He had no strength to get near Odysseus, who was so touched by the dog's devotion that he dropped a tear, unseen by any. At that moment Argos dropped dead upon the dung hill.

Eumaeus went straightway to sit beside his master Telemachus, who ordered that he should be given bread and meat. A minute later Odysseus, King of Ithaca, stepped inside his own hall, where he had not set foot for twenty years. In the guise of a filthy, travel-stained beggar in tattered rags he shuffled to the hearth and sat down in the ashes. In this way the lord of Ithaca made his homecoming. As soon as Telemachus saw him, he took up another plate of bread and meat and told Eumaeus to take it to Odysseus. Odysseus was told, when he had finished it, to take his bag round the hall and beg for scraps from the revellers.

Eumaeus did as he was bidden, and Odysseus, taking the food, called upon the gods to befriend Telemachus and give him all he desired. While the minstrel played on, Odysseus ate his food, and then prepared to go round the suitors asking for scraps to put in his wallet. The goddess Athene was to accompany him, invisible, and the two of them would observe each suitor in turn to see which were the villains and which the harmless ones. As Odysseus

went round among the suitors, some gave him morsels
of food out of pity, and many asked among themselves
who the stranger could be and where he came from.
Melanthius, the goat-herd then said he had already
seen the strange beggarman but that he knew nothing
of him. He had been brought to the palace by Eumaeus
the swine-herd.

Antinous looked at Eumaeus and spoke to him
scornfully.

"So it was you who brought this beggar to town and
to the palace. Have we not enough beggars in the town
already? And surely there are enough outsiders eating
and drinking at the expense of the palace without
adding this disreputable beggar to their company?"

"You are a hard man, Antinous," said Eumaeus,
"and you have always disliked me and everything I do.
Any man will bring a skilled craftsman or a fine
musician to a banquet; but someone must also take
care of humbler folk without skill who are down on
their luck."

"Don't answer Antinous," said Telemachus to the
swine-herd. "He enjoys being scurrilous about
humbler men who cannot argue with him."

But Telemachus himself turned to Antinous and
said sarcastically:

"You are like a father to me, my good Antinous,
looking after my welfare in this way. It is thoughtful
of you to see that my goods are not wasted. But I
do not grudge this beggar a morsel. You see what you
can give him. I give you my full permission. Now be
generous to him. He has done you no harm."

"Don't lose your temper, Telemachus," said
Antinous in his calm, disdainful drawl. "I will give the
beggar something, and if everyone here gave him what

I shall give him, that would be enough to keep him away for three months."

So saying, he removed his sleek feet from the footstool on which they were resting and picked it up with a threatening gesture, as if he were going to hit Odysseus. However, the other guests gave him plenty of scraps, so that he soon had a full wallet. Odysseus shouldered the wallet and made towards the door into the courtyard. He approached Antinous and spoke to him quietly and humbly.

"My friend," said he, "you alone have given me nothing. You have the air of a king. Be generous, I beg you, and give me something to put in my bag. You may not believe me, but I was once rich and handsome like you, and had land and goods, servants and riches. I often gave to beggars. They never went away empty-handed from *my* door."

Odysseus then began to tell Antinous the tale of how he had once been strong and prosperous and how he had lost his fortune and come to beggary. But Antinous would not listen.

"Keep your story for yourself, foul beggar," he interrupted. "Get away from here with all the speed you can, and stop spoiling our feast with your disgusting presence."

"Now I see," replied Odysseus, "that despite your noble appearance you are a mean, hard-hearted man. At your own home, wherever that may be, you would not give so much as a grain of salt to help a traveller in distress. Here, where you are enjoying another's food and drink, you could easily have spared a morsel."

"Insolent villain!" cried Antinous. "Here is something you may take as a present from me."

He lifted his footstool and aimed a blow at Odysseus, catching him on the back just below the right shoulder. Odysseus neither cried out nor flinched. He looked silently at Antinous, shaking his head. He brooded evil in his heart. Then he took his bag, went and sat down at the entrance to the hall and spoke to the suitors. "This proud and ill-mannered prince," he said, "has insulted me and shamed you all. So I swear before you all that, if there is justice between gods and men, destruction shall fall upon him before the day of his wedding. As the gods are my witness, I pray that this may be."

"Well, stranger," Antinous said, somewhat ashamed, "eat your bread in peace and leave us."

By this time the other suitors were heartily angry with Antinous and one of the younger men spoke to him.

"Antinous," he said sternly, "you did wrong to strike this stranger, and you did wrong to insult him. You are now a doomed man. You well know that the gods sometimes travel about among men to search out the good they do, and the evil. Perhaps they have witnessed your misdoings and will punish you."

Antinous ignored these words and took no notice of the reproaches of the suitors. Telemachus was infuriated by the attack on Odysseus, but he kept back the bitter tears that rose to his eyes. He must do nothing to reveal his knowledge of the beggar. When Penelope, who was upstairs with her women, heard that a stranger in her house had been struck, she came down and denounced Antinous, saying:

"May Apollo, the famous archer, strike you, Antinous, as you struck this stranger."

She turned to her women and added:

"And may I soon be rid of Antinous and of all other suitors."

Penelope then sent for Eumaeus and told him to bring the stranger before her.

"Perhaps he has heard news of Odysseus," she said. "For it seems he has travelled far. I would like to speak with him."

"Oh yes, indeed," Eumaeus answered eagerly. "It will give you joy to hear this stranger. For three days he has been my guest, and I have never heard tales like his. I think he has knowledge of Odysseus and was once a companion of his at Troy."

Penelope repeated her order to Eumaeus to send the beggar to talk with her.

"Oh," she cried, as the swine-herd left her, "if only it were possible for Odysseus to return at last and be revenged upon these greedy men who have for so long gorged themselves on the riches of our house."

Eumaeus went straight away to the beggar and told him to go and speak with his mistress Penelope.

"She wishes to hear your story," he said, "and especially to learn what you know of my master Odysseus."

Odysseus replied that if he should go once more through the hall, he might meet further ill-treatment by the suitors. Let the Queen remain upstairs with her women until nightfall. Then Odysseus would be ready to talk to her near the fireplace.

"Why are you alone?" asked Penelope, when she saw Eumaeus returning to her without the beggar.

"He will speak with you," said the swine-herd, "but he would rather wait till nightfall. It will be better for you to speak to him alone."

Penelope agreed that this was the wisest course. Then Eumaeus went and spoke in a low voice to Telemachus.

"I will go now," he said, "and see that your swine are all shut up safely. You are in charge here. First, look to your own safety, for you have many enemies. Then see that the stranger, whom I leave in your charge, comes to no harm."

Telemachus bade farewell to the swine-herd and told him to come back in the morning with fresh beasts for slaughter and sacrifice. So, after a last dish of meat and a bowl of wine, Eumaeus departed, leaving the hall loud with the singing and dancing of the young men. It was already nearing nightfall.

15

Odysseus fights with a beggar

THERE WAS AN insolent, loafing beggar, well known in Ithaca, who used to run errands for the suitors. He hung about the palace as if by right. His name was Irus. He looked tall and strong enough, but in truth he was a feeble creature. When he appeared at the palace, he saw Odysseus in the doorway.

"Back from there, old man!" called Irus contemptuously. "Back, I say, or I will drag you out by the heels."

Surprised by this greeting, Odysseus nevertheless answered the beggar peaceably.

"I have done you no wrong, friend. There is room for us both in this doorway."

"Away with you", went on Irus, "or I will throw you out, ashamed as I am to fight with such an old scarecrow as you."

"Mind what you say," Odysseus replied, his brow clouding with anger. "Old as I am, I can hit you hard enough to keep you away from the hall of Odysseus for some time."

"Listen to the old man," cried Irus, laughing contemptuously. "How he rambles on. I'm itching to get at him with my fists and knock out what teeth he has left in his gums. Strip yourself for the fight, old man, and let these lords see what I shall do."

Antinous, leader among the suitors, overheard the two beggars and cried:

"Come, friends. Let us see this sport. These two fellows have challenged each other to a fight. Let's make a ring and surround them."

He and his friends, roaring with laughter, gathered about the beggars and Antinous went on:

"There are the meat pies set aside for supper. Let the best man win, and he shall have the pick of them. He can eat with us every night for a week, and we will let no other come near us to ask for gifts."

Then Odysseus said craftily:

"Friends, I am an old man and no match for a young blade like this. But what can I do? I must fight for I am hungry. But I beg that none of you will strike me or lend a hand to help my opponent."

All agreed to Odysseus' request, and Telemachus added:

"Whoever hits you unfairly will have to reckon with me, for I am your host, and I will see fair play. I call upon Antinous and Eurymachus to do likewise."

Satisfied with these words, Odysseus pulled up his rags and tied them tight about his waist, showing his sturdy limbs, so that all the onlookers marvelled at the strength of the old man's muscles. Such a fellow, they thought, would be more than a match for the flabby, pot-bellied Irus. This beggar, on seeing his opponent's broad shoulders and strong thighs, trembled, but it was too late now. He hung back; so the lords' henchmen pushed him into the ring and made him face Odysseus. At first Odysseus was tempted to strike him dead at a blow, but he decided that this would be unwise. The lords might guess who he was, and it did not suit him to reveal himself so soon. So the two fighters put up their fists, and on the signal to begin, Odysseus struck Irus a heavy blow on the neck, crushing in the bones under the ear. Irus fell flat on the ground, groaning in the dust, while the suitors roared with delight. Irus showed no desire to go on with the fight, and Odysseus clutched him by the heel and dragged him out of the ring. He lifted him, propped him against the wall and put a staff in his hand.

"Stand here and guard over the swine," he said. "But don't try again to tell strangers what to do. If you try again to lord it over me, you'll not be let off so lightly next time."

Then Odysseus returned to the hall and took up his place again on the threshold. The lords shouted their applause and one said:

"May the gods give you all you wish for, stranger, as a reward for getting rid of that tiresome beggar."

Then Antinous put a huge meat pie in front of Odysseus, and another of the suitors, a young man named Amphinomus, brought him bread and wine. This Amphinomus was a gentle youth, and Odysseus could see that he had no evil in his heart. So he drew close to him as he drank the wine and said to him in a low voice:

"Let me give you a warning, young man. Men are weak creatures and believe that, while they have strength, no harm can befall them. But they are subject to the will of the gods, and no man is safe. So it was with me. When I had youth and strength, I trusted in myself and my wealth and my kinfolk and committed many wrongs. Now you see that I am come to beggary in my old age. So it will be, I tell you, with these lords. They are insulting the wife and

K

eating up the wealth of a man they think they will never see again. But I tell you, friend, he is not so far away. He will not be long in coming, and when he comes, he will not again leave this house without bloodshed. May the gods preserve you and keep you safe. Go back to your home while there is yet time."

With these words he finished the cup of wine and handed it back to Amphinomus. The young man walked sadly through the hall. He shook his head distractedly from side to side, and his mind was full of foreboding. In spite of his kind heart and the warning of Odysseus, he could not escape the doom that was to fall on all the suitors alike in that place.

While this was going on, Penelope was, as usual, in her room, hearing the sound of revelling among the suitors. It came into her mind that she would show herself to them, although she hated the sight of them. She laughed a bitter laugh and told one of her servants to send two of her maidens to her to go with her into the hall, for she could not go alone. The servant went off to do her mistress's bidding, and Penelope lay down on her bed. Her protector Athene sent a deep sleep over her. Her head sank back and her body rested in slumber, while the goddess gave her new beauty. She seemed to grow taller and whiter than ever, so that she appeared like a goddess. Then her maidens came in, and the queen awoke at the sound of their voices.

"What a sweet sleep came over me," she said drowsily, rubbing her eyes. "Oh, if only the sleep of death could fall upon me so gently, that I might finish this weary life of longing for my lost husband."

The maidens led her down to the hall. She stood in the doorway with a veil over her face. All the suitors gazed upon her, wondering at her beauty. Each of them longed to win her for himself. Eurymachus spoke.

"Lady," he said, "if all the Greeks could see you now, there would be still more suitors thronging your hall, for of all women on earth you are the fairest."

"Eurymachus," Penelope answered wearily, "the day my husband sailed with the Greeks to Troy, the gods took away all my beauty. I shall never forget how, as we parted, he laid his hand on mine and said: 'There are many good men at Troy, swordsmen and spearmen, and many of us Greeks will never come home again. What will happen to me I cannot tell, but I leave everything in your care—my palace, my servants, my goods, but above all, my dear father and mother, whom you must care for more than ever, now that I am going. But when my son Telemachus, now a baby, is grown to manhood, you may leave all this and take another husband. If I have not returned, you may marry whom you please.' Well now, you see, Eurymachus, everything has turned out as he said. The black day must come soon when I must make the marriage that I hate. But I tell you, I am displeased at the treatment I receive from my wooers. It was once the custom that when men courted a king's daughter, they brought her rich gifts and made feasts for her and her kinsfolk, instead of devouring her wealth and consuming what did not belong to them."

So Penelope spoke, with anger and scorn in her voice, and Odysseus in his beggar's guise smiled to himself as he heard how his wife spoke to the lords.

Then Antinous answered:

"You are right. We have gifts for you, and we beg you to accept them. It is proper that you should expect presents from us. But we mean to stay here until you have accepted the best man among us in marriage."

The rest of the suitors agreed with the words of Antinous, and heralds were sent to fetch the gifts: from one there was an embroidered robe with twelve golden clasps; from another a golden necklace set with amber beads; from others bracelets and ear-rings, and many sumptuous gifts besides. Then Penelope went back to her room, and her maids followed with the presents. Meanwhile, the lords danced, sang and made merry until the coming of evening.

As darkness began to fall, the servants came in with baskets full of logs and made a fire in the hearth.

"Go back to your mistress," said Odysseus. "I will stay here and look after the fire. You will be able to cheer the Queen with your talk; I will stay up as long as your guests are here. I can keep awake till dawn if necessary. I have been through many hardships."

Then Melantha, the most forward and insolent of the girls, said:

"You should be begging in the market-place, stranger, or working for my mistress out in the smithy. But here you sit talking and idling your time away. Perhaps you have got a swollen head because you beat Irus. But a better man than he will come and throw you out of doors."

"You are a saucy wench," said Odysseus, glaring at Melantha from under his shaggy brow. "I will tell Telemachus what you say, and he will have you put to death."

At this the maids were scared. They ran from the hall, leaving Odysseus watching the fire and thinking about the great vengeance which was to come.

But it was not yet time for the goddess Athene

to take the part of Odysseus against the suitors. He must put up with further insults first. Eurymachus began mocking the beggar, sneering at his rough and ragged appearance, to make the other lords laugh. Then he said to Odysseus:

"You are a sturdy fellow. Would you like to come and work on my farm for me? You could plant trees and build walls. I would pay you a handsome wage, and give you food and clothing as well. But what is the use of asking? You have learned bad ways and are only fit for begging and sponging on others."

Odysseus looked hard at Eurymachus and said to him, slowly and gravely:

"If I could challenge you in the Spring at a ploughing match, or reaping, I would show you I am as good a man as you. Or if some enemy came upon us all in this place and I could lay hands on a bronze helmet, a shield and spear, you would see that I could fight as well as you or anyone else here."

Then Odysseus added, his voice rising somewhat in anger:

"Yes, you would have no cause then to make fun of my rags and my hunger. You think you are strong, Eurymachus, because everyone about you is weak. I tell you this—if Odysseus were to come to his home again this day, these doors, though they are broad enough, would be too narrow to let you and your guzzling friends escape."

Eurymachus, flushed with rage, seized a footstool and flung it full at Odysseus; but Odysseus stepped nimbly aside and the stool struck a cup-bearer on the hand. Then there was a clamour in the hall, and the lords cried out against Odysseus.

"Curse the beggar!" they cried. "Why did he have

to come here to trouble us? Here we sit quarrelling over beggars, and the feast gives us no joy. A curse upon all idle beggars and boasters!"

"Sirs," said Telemachus, "you are drunk and cannot carry your liquor. I have no power to order you from the house, but my advice to you all is that you make an end of supper and go home for the night. There you can sleep off your wine."

"You have spoken well," said Amphinomous, and he ordered the herald to make an end of the feast. They did this, and the lords went away, each to his own place.

Then Odysseus was left alone in the hall with Telemachus.

"We have work to do," he said. "Let us put away all the weapons. If the princes notice they are missing, you can say they have been taken to the armoury to be cleaned and burnished since they have tarnished in the smoke from the fire."

Telemachus accordingly sent to the women's quarters for the old nurse Eurycleia and told her to keep the women out of the way while he put away all his father's weapons.

"They have been too long exposed to the wood smoke in the hall," he said.

"I will do as you say," said Eurycleia gladly. "I am pleased you show such care for your father's possessions."

As soon as the nurse had gone, Telemachus and his father took the bronze helmets, the shields and spears from their places on the walls and carried them out of the hall. Athene was with them, and she shed a clear golden light about the two men so that they could see to do their work. Athene was herself invisible, and

Telemachus marvelled at the golden light which gleamed on the walls and pillars of the hall and on the bronze weapons.

"Father," he said, "is there not a god with us who sends this unearthly light?"

"Ask no questions, my son," Odysseus answered. "Keep this vision in your heart. Question not the work of the immortals. Now you must go and get some sleep. I will stay here a while, for I must speak to your mother and the women."

Telemachus went off to his room, and soon Penelope came in, attended by her women. They set out her ivory and silver chair, with a footstool for her feet. Penelope made them put a stool beside her own, with a soft fleece on it for Odysseus. They did this, and then set to work to clear away the dishes after the evening's feast. When the servants had retired, Penelope said to Odysseus, now seated beside her:

"Stranger, tell me who you are and where you come from."

But Odysseus was not yet ready to reveal himself. He deliberately avoided his wife's question and said:

"Gracious lady, I think there is no one in he world who would not praise you. Your fame is like that of a just and prosperous king. Do not, therefore, ask questions about *my* country, for its condition would only bring sorrow to both our hearts. I am one who has had many troubles, and I do not care to mourn and lament for myself in the hall of another."

"Stranger," answered Penelope, "all my honour and beauty left me the day my husband went away. That was twenty years ago, and ever since then I have neglected the claims of guests and kinsfolk and spend my nights and days sorrowing for him. The lords and princes of Ithaca and other islands nearby woo me, much against my will. I have put them all off, year after year, and now I can think of no more ways to refuse them. My parents would have me take a second husband, and my son Telemachus, who has now grown to manhood, is angry at seeing the waste of all his inheritance. But now tell me of yourself."

Odysseus told her a long tale of how he had lived prosperously in Crete until he had taken to war and wandering. He told how, many years before, he had entertained Odysseus in Crete, and at this Penelope's tears began to flow. She wept at the memory of the very man who was sitting beside her. Pity gushed into the heart of Odysseus, but he forced back his feelings. It was not time, he told himself, to say who he was, and he compelled himself to harden his heart. Soon enough it would be time to show his love.

When Penelope had dried her tears, she said:

"Now stranger, you say you saw my husband face to face. I will put you to the test and see if you speak the truth. Tell me how he looked, what his clothes were and who were his companions."

"It is difficult to remember after all these years," replied Odysseus. "Nearly twenty have passed since I saw him, but I will search my memory and tell you all I can. Let me see."

Here Odysseus hesitated, pretending to search far into the past.

"He wore a thick, purple robe," he said, "clasped with a brooch of silver—no, it was gold, and on it was engraved the image of a hound holding in its mouth a spotted fawn. I noticed particularly his doublet too, for it was uncommonly glossy, as if it had been polished. There was in his company a herald, somewhat older than he—round-shouldered, dark-skinned, with curly hair. Odysseus paid special attention to this man and gave him more honour than all the others."

At this Penelope wept afresh.

"Dear stranger," she said between her sobs, "from the first I have pitied you, but now I honour and reverence you. That was indeed Odysseus. It was I who wrought the cloak and doublet and fastened the gold brooch on his breast. I shall never see him again, but weep for the rest of my life over the accursed day when he sailed for the evil city of Troy."

"Gracious Queen," answered Odysseus, "do not wear out your heart with grieving. Not long ago, when I was in Epirus, I heard news of Odysseus. True, he had lost all his companions, drowned beneath the stormy waves, for they had angered the gods. But he himself is safe, and I swear to you, by those same gods, that he will return to you this very year—yes, even before the next moon is full."

"Alas, stranger," said Penelope, "I am grateful for your care and your hope, but my heart misgives me. Now, let my maids wash your feet and prepare a bed for you. Tomorrow you shall sit next to my son Telemachus, and none of the insolent lords shall be allowed to touch you. If I allowed such a guest as you to sit dishonoured in my house, how could men call me wise?"

"I am used to lying on a hard bed," answered Odysseus, "so I will lie tonight. I do not desire that any of your maids shall wash my feet. But if there is some old and trusted woman in the house, such as has borne sorrows like mine I would let her come and wash me and prepare me for sleep."

"Indeed, stranger," Penelope replied, "there is such

a woman in the house, old, faithful and trusted. She carried Odysseus in her arms many times when he was a baby. It is she whom I will send to wash your feet."

So she called Eurycleia to her and asked her to attend on the stranger. The old nurse had been listening to Penelope's words, and at the mention of Odysseus she had covered her face in her apron and wept.

"Oh, my dear, dear Odysseus," she moaned, "there was no man who ever honoured the gods more than he did; yet they have not allowed him to return to his home. If he lives at all, he is in some far off place, treated as a beggar, and the women mock him."

Odysseus smiled secretly to himself, and Eurycleia went on:

"Yes, stranger, I will gladly attend on you, for my heart is drawn to you. Of all the guests who have come to our house in all these years, none has been more like my master Odysseus in face, in voice and in bearing."

"Yes, indeed," said Odysseus, still smiling inwardly, "you have the right to say I am like Odysseus, for you have seen the two of us."

The nurse brought a basin of water and a towel, and Odysseus turned quickly away from the light of the fire, for fear that Eurycleia might recognise him by the sight of an old scar on his thigh where a tusked boar had gashed him as a boy. For he did not yet desire that the truth should be known as to who he really was. But as she washed him, Eurycleia passed her hand over the scar. She knew it instantly. She dropped his foot, and the basin was overturned and all the water spilt. Such was the amazement of the old woman as she knew all of a sudden who the stranger was. Sorrow and

a great joy fought together in her heart. The tears
welled up, and she cried with a strangled sob:

"You are he, my dearest child. I did not know it
until I touched you with my own hands."

She looked at Penelope, who was sitting in her chair
at some distance. She longed to tell her the news, but
Penelope noticed nothing, for her thoughts had been
turned away from the nurse and the stranger by the
goddess Athene.

"Nurse," said Odysseus in a quiet, urgent voice,
putting his hand over her mouth. "Be quiet, or you
will be the death of me. Be silent and tell no one in the
house—no one, I say,—what you have seen. Otherwise
I will have no mercy on you when the day of recognition
comes."

"You need not speak to me like that, my child,"
softly answered Eurycleia. "You know that I will be
as silent as death. Not a word of this shall escape me."

"Keep silence, then," Odysseus murmured, "and leave everything to the gods."

Then the old nurse brought fresh water and washed Odysseus' feet and rubbed in oil. Odysseus covered the scar on his leg and drew his stool nearer to the fire.

"Stranger," said Penelope, "there is no more matter on which I would ask your advice. I do not know whether I should stay here with my son Telemachus or whether I should marry one of these lords and go elsewhere with him. Let me tell you a dream which came to me, and you shall interpret it. In my courtyard I have twenty geese, who feed on wheat from an oaken trough. In my dream a fierce eagle swooped down from the mountains and killed all my geese as I looked at them. I wept bitterly over them as they lay on the ground with their necks broken. But the eagle perched on a beam overhanging the courtyard and spoke to me with a human voice. 'Penelope,' the eagle said, 'what you have seen is no dream but a true vision of what will happen here. These geese are your suitors, and I am your husband, come to take vengeance upon them.' At these words I awoke and ran to the window. There in the courtyard were my geese, pecking up the wheat grains just as before. The eagle was nowhere to be seen."

"Madam," answered Odysseus, who had been listening intently to his wife's tale, "there is only one way to explain this dream. It is as if Odysseus himself had interpreted your dream."

"Well," answered Penelope, "dreams are always of doubtful meaning. We can never be certain what they forebode. But now, stranger, listen to what I have resolved. Tomorrow I will make my suitors show which of them is the best. I remember how my lord

Odysseus used to shoot an arrow through twelve axes in a row, with holes pierced in their blades. I will make the suitors take the bow of Odysseus and perform the same feat as he used to do. The first of these lords who can do this shall win the contest and take me away from this house as his bride. I shall never forget the fair house full of fine treasures to which my husband brought me when he married me."

"Lady," answered Odysseus, "let it be as you say, and let the trial be held without delay. Odysseus will be here before any of them bends that bow."

Then Penelope told her servants to prepare a couch for her guest to lie on. She herself went up to her own room and wept piteously until she fell asleep. She had made her decision, and she knew that her fate would be decided on the morrow.

16

The bending of the bow

ODYSSEUS LAY IN the porch outside the hall, but the doubt and anger fighting in his breast would not let him sleep. He turned and tossed this way and that, asking himself how he could do battle against his foes. How could one man ever hope to succeed against so many? His case seemed hopeless. And as he lay in a fever of despair, his protecting goddess Athene came and stood beside him, now in the likeness of a living woman.

She laid her hand gently on his hot forehead and said:

"Must you be for ever restless, my son? This is your own home, and your own beloved wife is within. Telemachus is here too, a young man worthy to be the son of a hero."

"You say true, goddess," answered Odysseus wearily, "but my mind can see no way in which I can fight these princes. I am one and they a host. Even supposing that, with the aid of the immortal gods I should achieve the miracle of killing or routing them, surely great vengeance will later fall on my head and my household."

"O fearful heart," said the grey-eyed Athene quietly, "other men put their trust in mortal friends. I am a goddess and have guarded you in all your dangers. I have been with you ever since the days of Troy. Shall I desert you now? You shall conquer all your foes, even if there were fifty companies of them. Sleep, Odysseus. The end of all your trouble is not far off, but now you have need of rest."

The grey-eyed goddess returned to her home in Mount Olympus, leaving Odysseus asleep.

Indoors the slumber of Penelope was broken by tears. She wept for her husband and was so distressed that she prayed to the gods to let her die. She did not yet know that her husband had returned to his own hall, and she had determined that on the morrow she would give in to her doom—the doom of forgetting Odysseus for ever and taking another husband.

When Odysseus woke at early dawn, with the first birds carolling in the trees, he heard Penelope's voice inside the house. It seemed as if she were already standing at his bedside to give him fresh heart.

In the courtyard stood a great stone altar dedicated to Zeus. Odysseus jumped up and went straight to the altar, where he knelt in prayer.

"O mighty Zeus," he said, raising his hands to heaven, "Chief of the immortal gods, give me a sign, so that I may truly know that it is you who have brought me through all my perils and made me reach the end of my long journey."

Even as he prayed, his thoughts were bitter and revengeful, and he was tempted to rush into the house, while all were asleep, and with his sharp sword slay as many of the suitors as had stayed the night there, snoring away their drunkenness upon the rugs.

At the very moment when Odysseus finished his prayer to Zeus, there sounded in the sky a single mighty thunder clap. It so happened that in a corner of the yard a poor maidservant had been grinding corn all night long, until she was ready to drop with weariness. When she heard the thunder, she stopped turning the millstone and said: "Not a cloud in the sky—yet there is thunder. That must be a sign from the gods, for is not Zeus lord of the thunder and the lightning? I have worn out my strength grinding grain, day and night, for the feasts of those guzzling princes. I pray with all my might that this feast may be their last."

Odysseus heard the thunderclap and the words of the girl. He rejoiced in his heart, for now he knew that the long-awaited day of vengeance had dawned. The household was already astir. In the hall the other servants were lighting the fire. Telemachus came in and spoke to Eurycleia.

"Has the stranger been well looked after, nurse? My mother is not always as careful of strangers as she should be."

"Your mother treated him with the greatest favour," replied the old woman. "She gave him wine, but he refused food. He slept on a rough bed in the porch, it is true, but that was his own wish."

Telemachus smiled with satisfaction and, calling to his two dogs, went off to the city. Eurycleia and the maids prepared the hall, spreading skins and fleeces on the stools. The serving men brought in logs for the fire. Eumaeus, as he had been ordered, arrived with three fat swine, the finest in his herd. He spoke to Odysseus asking how he had been treated by the suitors. Odysseus told him of their rudeness and of the fight with Irus, the beggar. Melanthius, the insolent goat-herd, came into the courtyard, driving goats for the banquet. He once more insulted Odysseus, still believing him to be a ragged beggar. He would have drawn Odysseus into a fight, but Odysseus refused to answer him. This was no time to be picking quarrels with foul-mouthed goat-herds. Then a labourer called Philoetius came along, driving before him a heifer for sacrifice. He was a loyal friend to the people at the palace—Penelope and the household of Odysseus. He went over to Eumaeus, looking keenly at Odysseus, and asked:

"Who is that man? In spite of his rags, he looks like a king."

Then he clasped Odysseus' weathered hand firmly and said:

"May all your troubles end happily, old man. You are welcome, though it brings tears to my eyes to look on you. You remind me of my master Odysseus, who put me in charge of his bulls and his cows when I was a boy. I have minded them ever since, just as if Odysseus himself were here. They have multiplied and grown in strength, so that you could not find a better herd in all the islands. Yet, friend, my herd gives me no joy, for they are consumed daily by this horde of princes. My fate is past bearing. I would long ago have taken service with another master in another place, but that I think all the time of my master and the troubles of his house. I pray always that he may come back and drive out these strangers."

"Well spoken, friend," replied Odysseus. "Now listen to what I say. Only wait a little longer, and I promise you that your master will return. With your own eyes you shall witness the end of these lords. Here they come." As he spoke, the first of the princes, chattering and laughing, swaggered into the courtyard and strolled through the door into the hall. They seated themselves at the tables, to await the feast. Telemachus

L

saw to it that Odysseus came into the hall. He had a low stool placed for him just inside the stone threshold; a small table stood before it. He brought him food and drink, saying:

"Take your place, stranger, without fear. There will be no roistering and no disorder here. It is the house of Odysseus and my inheritance."

"Let him have his say," Antinous said to some of the suitors who had heard the young man. "If Zeus had not interfered with our plans, we'd have shut his bragging mouth for ever."

Then another of the suitors stood up, taking a marrowbone from one of the dishes.

"Your friend shall have his share of the feast, Telemachus," he shouted. "Here is my contribution."

He flung the bone at Odysseus. But the King ducked his head, and the bone hit the wall behind him. Odysseus grimaced severely to himself. Telemachus stood up and said with firm and dignified authority:

"It is a good thing for you that your bone missed its mark. If you had hit my guest, I would have run my spear through your body. There would have been no marriage at your father's house, but a funeral and the sound of lamentation. Let there be an end of brawling. I am no longer a boy. I am a man and will have no more disorder and insolence."

"Quite right, young fellow," said one of the suitors. "You do well to protect a stranger at our feast. But you must listen to us. As long as there was a chance of your father's return, it was fair that you should put us off and keep us waiting. But now it is clear to everyone that he will never come back. So go to your mother and tell her she must choose a husband from among us."

Telemachus answered:

"Let my mother make what choice she will. I will not interfere."

Then a strange and terrible thing took place in the hall. Athene spread a fever of madness among the suitors, who began to laugh uncontrollably, like men in a hysteria. The expression on their faces changed, and the meat on their plates sweated with blood. Their eyes filled with tears and they sobbed even as they laughed. In the midst of the confusion the prophet Theoclymenus stood up and called out in the high, strained voice of one foretelling a terrible disaster:

"O unfortunate souls—souls of the doomed. What mania has come upon you? Darkness has fallen upon your heads and upon your knees. Your cheeks run with tears. The walls are stained with red blood, and I hear the sound of wailing and lamentation. The porch and the courtyard are crowded with spirits, hastening down to the black underworld. The sun is blotted from the sky, and a thick mist covers the earth."

The princes only laughed the more hysterically, and Eurymachus said between his sobs:

"This man is mad. Lead the fellow out into the market place, if he can see nothing in here."

"I need no help from you, Eurymachus," cried the prophet. "I have eyes and ears of my own, and understanding. I can see what is hidden from other men. Nevertheless, I will leave this place, for I witness the coming of a fearful doom. None of you shall escape it who wanton and riot in the house of King Odysseus."

With these words, he gathered his cloak about him and left the palace. But the lords paid him no more heed, and one of them mocked Telemachus, saying:

"You have little luck with your guests, young man.

First you entertain a beggarly wanderer who is no good either for work or for fighting. Then you have a madman, standing up in our midst and prophesying woe. Let them be sold as slaves. It is all they are fit for."

Telemachus said never a word. He sat in silence and with as much calm as he could. He looked towards Odysseus, and waited the moment for action.

Penelope meanwhile sat behind the closed door of the women's room at the back of the hall. To her ears came the sound of talking and jesting and the strange hysterical laughter, mingled with sobbing, which had come over the suitors. She heard the high, strained voice of the prophet, but she could not catch his words. Then it came into Penelope's mind to bring out Odysseus' great bow and begin the competition for her hand in marriage. She beckoned to some of her women, who went with her to the treasury where the wealth of her house was stored. There hung the ceremonial gold helmets, the bronze shields, the spears of iron. There hung the keen arrows, bunched in their quiver of leather, decorated with silver ornaments. And there hung the great bow given to Odysseus long ago by one of the Greek heroes. With a heavy heart, where no hope breathed, Odysseus' wife took down the bow and slowly drew it out of the polished bow-case. She sank on to a stool, laid the bow over her knees and sobbed quietly. Then she dried her eyes and went into the hall to see the suitors. Attendants followed her, carrying over their shoulders the twelve pierced axes.

Penelope stood in the doorway, holding her veil in front of her face. The princes fell silent, all eyes turned towards her. She said in clear tones, with no faltering:

"Lords and princes, you have feasted and revelled in

my house all these long years, while my husband was away from home. Your only excuse for living at my expense and abusing my hospitality was that you were my suitors. Well, here at last is the prize you seek."

She paused a moment, then continued in a voice of cold disdain.

"Here is the famous bow of Odysseus, which none of you has seen before but of which all the world knows. It was the gift of a hero who honoured my husband. To whomever of you can bend this bow and string it and shoot an arrow through the pierced heads of twelve axes in a row—to him will I give myself in marriage. My husband could perform this feat, and no man who cannot do the same is worthy of me."

An awed silence greeted Penelope's words. So now the choice was to be made. After these years of waiting, the wooing was to end. One of the suitors was to be made husband to the gracious and honourable widow of Odysseus. Penelope told the swine-herd to take the bow and to see to the setting up of the axes in a row. Holding his master's weapon, Eumaeus shed tears over it. The cow-herd wept too, remembering Odysseus. Antinous spoke to them with rude scorn:

"Why do you snivel over the bow, miserable slaves? It will only upset your mistress. Get outside, Cry there, and leave the bow to us. We shan't find it easy to draw it, for none of us is as strong as Odysseus was. I remember him well, though I was only a boy when he left Ithaca."

But Antinous smiled with inward triumph, secretly believing that he could bend the bow. Next Telemachus stood up and said he would himself try to bend the bow, and that if he won, his mother need take no suitor and need not leave her home. He drew a straight line in the earth floor right down the centre of the hall. With this as a guide he dug a narrow trench with a mattock which one of the servants had been ordered to have ready. In this trench he planted the twelve axes in a row, with the holes through their blades all in a line. He and Eumaeus stamped down the earth firmly about the hafts.

All eyes were on the young man as he strove to bend the bow and so save his mother from the fate she feared. He saw that the long shaft had been well preserved with oil and resin and that the slack leather string had been well preserved with pig's grease. He grasped the shaft with his strong left hand at the centre and took the string in his right hand. Three times he strained to bend the haft far enough to notch the string over the end of the bow. Each time he got a little nearer to success. At the fourth attempt he would perhaps have succeeded, but he caught Odysseus' eye as he sat on his stool by the door. Odysseus shook his head very slightly, and Telemachus knew that his father had forbidden the attempt. He laid down the bow on one of the tables, saying, as he strained to get his breath back:

"I am still too young for a task like this. Now let us see which of you is stronger than I. Take up my father's bow and finish the match."

"Good," cried Antinous. "Let us all try, in the order in which we sit: and you, priest, begin."

Without a word the priest went and took up the bow. His fine hands, unused to athletic deeds, had no strength in them, and he could not bend it. He replaced the bow on the table and said:

"Let the next man try. I am afraid even the

strongest among us may fail. Give up the struggle and court some other woman. If the wife of Odysseus is to marry again, her husband will be sent by the fates."

Antinous jumped up.

"Because you cannot bend the bow, must we all despair?" he asked angrily. "You were never an archer, but there are some here who will do the task easily. You, goat-herd Melanthius, heap logs on to the fire and let us have a blaze. Then fetch lard from the kitchen, so that we can grease the bow. No doubt it is stiff from long disuse and must be made supple."

Lard was brought, and the youngest princes all tried in turn. Sweat and strain as they might, none could string the bow. At last only two were left. Antinous and Eurymachus reserved their strength, and they were the strongest of all the wooers. Disdainfully they had watched their younger companions' prowess, and now it was their turn. Then, while the company began to look towards Antinous and Eurymachus, Odysseus slipped out and was followed by Eumaeus and Philoetius, the cow-herd. When the three of them were out of sight of the hall, Odysseus said in a low and earnest voice:

"Tell me something: if a god were to bring Odysseus back this very instant, on whose side would you be, the suitors' or Odysseus? There would be a battle. For whom would you fight? Look me in the face and speak truly."

"Oh that Odysseus might come," answered the cow-herd without hesitation. "Then you would see how my strong arm would come to his help."

The swine-herd immediately echoed the other's words. Then, taking a hand of each of them in his own, Odysseus spoke.

"I am Odysseus," he said quietly. "I am the very man, and here I stand, outside my own home. Now you are the only two among my old servants who has welcomed me. I promise you, upon my honour and my trust in the gods, that if I conquer these princes, I will love you as I love my own son."

Stepping back, Odysseus drew aside his rags and showed them the scar on his leg which the boar's tusk had made when he was young. There it was, a broad, curving mark, smooth and white, running down his left thigh, almost to the knee. At once the two loyal servants recognised their master. They threw their arms about him, kissed him and wept for pleasure. Tears of thanksgiving ran down their cheeks.

"Do not weep now," Odysseus said. "Someone may come from the hall and see us. Keep your feelings till later. We must go back into the palace. I shall go first, and you will slip back singly after me. Listen carefully:

I will give you a signal, and this is it. I shall demand the bow. The suitors will forbid me to have it, but you must obey me. Eumaeus, you will carry the bow down the hall and give it into my hands. Then go at once to the women and tell them to go back into their room. If they hear sounds of fighting, they are not to come out. Meanwhile, Philoetius, it will be your task to go swiftly into the courtyard here and shut the gates. Make them fast by whatever means you can, so that none may get through."

The two men nodded but said nothing. They had well understood their orders, and their master knew they would obey. Odysseus turned and shuffled back to his stool by the hall door. Soon afterwards Eumaeus and Philoetius followed, first one and then the other.

In the hall Eurymachus had taken the bow and rubbed pig's grease on the shaft. He warmed it by the fire, tested it and tried to bend it. In the dead silence the watchers could hear the straining of his tendons, but they saw no movement in the bow. Sweat poured from the forehead and chest of Eurymachus. Strong as he was, he too failed the test and flung the weapon down in his rage.

"Shame upon me and upon us all!" he cried bitterly. "I care nothing for the marriage. There are women in plenty in Ithaca and the other islands. I can get a wife anywhere. But it will never be forgotten that we have none of us the strength of Odysseus and are too feeble even to bend his bow. As long as time shall last, we will be spoken of with scorn and ridicule."

Antinous spoke:

"Do not be downhearted, friend Eurymachus," he said consolingly. "Things are not so bad as you say. Have you forgotten that today is the festival of Apollo—Apollo, the very god of archery? Who could expect us mortal men to bend a hero's bow on such a day? Lay down Odysseus' bow and leave the twelve axes in position. No one will take them. Tomorrow, early in the morning, we will make Melanthius bring along the finest goats in his herd as a sacrifice to Apollo. Then let us try our strength once more."

All listened favourably to Antinous, and there were murmurs of agreement. But Odysseus got to his feet and said, in grave, quiet tones—and there was something in his voice that compelled the princes to listen to him:

"Great princes, let me be heard, I beg you. Since none of you intends to try to bend the bow this day, let me try it. I would dearly love to see if I have

any of the strength left which I had as a younger man
and a warrior. Perhaps I have lost it all in my years of
battling with the wind and the sea."

At this request there were cries of anger. Some of
the lords feared in their secret hearts that this sturdy
beggar might succeed in bending the bow and putting
them all to shame. After all, he had fared hard and
had not been softened, like some of them, by years of
easy living at another's expense. Some, indeed, had
grown fat and short of breath.

Antinous broke out in a rage:

"Be quiet, fool! Is it not enough for you that you are
allowed to sit in our hall and listen to the conversation
of princes? Even if you *did* bend the bow, it would do
you no good. Drink your wine and do not measure
your strength against the strength of younger and
nobler men."

At these words it was Penelope's turn to raise her
voice.

"Antinous," she said icily, "you must not insult a
guest in this hall, the guest of Telemachus, son of
Odysseus. Even if this stranger should succeed in
bending the bow, there would be no question of his
taking me as his wife. No. He cannot hope for it
himself, so you need not fear it."

"You are right, Penelope," put in Eurymachus.
"There is no fear that this stranger will marry you.
That is not what troubles us. Our anxiety is lest it
should be said that we, the princes of Ithaca and
Greece, were too feeble to bend a bow which an old
ragged beggar has bent. So people would talk, and we
should lose honour."

"Eurymachus," Penelope answered, "it is not in
that way that you will lose your honour. This stranger

is tall and well-built. He says he comes of an honourable family. Give him the bow and let us see how strong he is. If he shoots from it, I will give him a cloak, a doublet, a good sword and a spear. He shall have new sandals for his feet, and I will send him wherever he desires to go."

"Mother," broke in Telemachus, "the bow is mine and only I have the right to give it or not to give it. If I choose to give it to this stranger to keep, none of the princes—no lord in all Greece—has the power to stop me. Go now, to your own quarters—you and the women. We men shall stay here and decide what is to be done with the bow. Go and do your women's tasks, I demand. I alone am master in this hall."

Penelope looked keenly at her son, but said nothing. He spoke sternly, almost harshly, but she heard in his tone a new authority and a new resolution. She went out of the hall and up to her room. She lay down on the bed where Athene sent swift sleep upon her.

Meanwhile Eumaeus the swine-herd took up the great bow, but the princes seized it from him and laid it down.

"Bring the bow to me, Eumaeus," called Telemachus angrily, "or I will turn you out of the house. Would to god I could get rid of these lords as easily as I can get rid of you!"

At these words the suitors laughed, and Eumaeus took up the bow, carried it down the hall and handed it to Telemachus. Then the swine-herd called Eurycleia out and said to her, speaking in a low voice, close to her ear:

"Telemachus orders you to see that the doors of the women's rooms are closed and barred. None is to come out. If they should hear cries or the sound of fighting,

they are on no account to look out. They must stay
within and go on with their work."

Eurycleia hurried to do as she was told, shutting
and barring the inner doors, so that none could pass
through from the hall. At the same time the cow-herd
Philotius carried out the orders Odysseus had given
him. He left the hall, went across the courtyard and
closed the gates. With a ship's cable that lay near to
hand, he tied the gates and made them fast. This he
did without attracting attention from inside the hall.
He returned to his place there and sat watching
Odysseus. While these things were being done,
Telemachus gave the bow into his father's hands, and
Odysseus, taking his time, examined the weapon
carefully. He wanted to see if any harm had come to
it during its long disuse, and whether worms had got
into the wood.

"This ruffian has a good eye for a bow," remarked
one of the lords. "Perhaps he has one like it at home."

But another of the lords said, shrugging his
shoulders:

"If the fellow can bend that bow, he can have anything he wants." Every eye was upon the stranger.
Odysseus had examined the bow in every detail. Now
he was ready. With no more trouble than a lute-player
fitting a new cord to his instrument, he bent the great
bow and looped the leather string into the notch at
the top of the shaft. He held the bow in his left hand
and plucked the string with his right. It sang beneath
his fingers as true and clear as the note of a swallow.
At this sound Zeus sent forth a peal of thunder.
Odysseus' heart leaped to hear it, but fear fell on all
the lords. Their faces went as pale as lard. Odysseus
paid no heed to them but swiftly took up an arrow,

laid it across the centre of the shaft, notched its end into the string, took aim and shot. The bronze-capped arrow went clean through the twelve holes in the axes. The princes let out their breath in amazement. Some whistled, others groaned, and some could not keep back a murmur of applause. In a ringing voice, for everyone to hear, Odysseus said:

"Telemachus, your guest has not disgraced you. I have hit the mark, and I took little time to do it. The hour has come. We have little daylight left, but we must give these princes their supper. Let there be dancing and singing too!"

At the words 'The hour has come' Telemachus knew his signal. He unsheathed his shining sword and grasped his spear.

17

The slaying of the suitors

THEN ODYSSEUS TORE off his ragged cloak and leapt upon the threshold of the hall with his great bow and his quiver full of arrows. He spilled the arrows upon the floor at his feet and raised his voice in triumph and defiance.

"At last," he cried, "the contest is over. Now I will aim at a mark which has never been hit before."

He fitted an arrow to the bow and pointed it full at Antinous, most powerful and most hated of the suitors. Antinous was even then raising to his lips a two-handled golden bowl of wine. Nothing was farther from his thoughts than death. The arrow struck Antinous full in the throat and passed through his neck. The wine cup dropped from his hand and dropped to the floor with a clang. He fell sideways, grasping the table, which toppled over. The bread and the roast meat slid to the floor and were fouled with the blood which spurted from Antinous' nose.

At the death of their leader, the wooers were afraid and raised a great clamour in the hall. They jumped from their seats and instantly looked about for weapons to defend themselves. But not a spear nor a shield, not a helmet nor a breastplate was hanging on the walls. Had not Telemachus and his father hidden them all the night before? So the princes turned upon Odysseus to curse him.

"Stranger," they cried, "your treachery shall be your downfall. Never again shall you fight among honest men. You have slain the noblest of the princes of Ithaca. You yourself shall be killed and the vultures shall gnaw your flesh."

"You dogs," Odysseus cried in defiance, "you said that I should never more return from Troy. You treacherously devoured my substance and paid court to my wife while I was still alive. You gave no heed to the anger of the gods who rule in heaven nor the scorn of men in after times. Now you are doomed, all of you."

At these words the suitors turned pale with terror and began to look about for means of escape. Eurymachus alone answered.

"If indeed you are Odysseus," he said in smooth, endearing tones, "what you say of us is true, and you have been deeply wronged. But Antinous our leader is slain. He it was who hoped to become lord of all Ithaca. He it was who persuaded us others to live at your expense and pay court to your noble wife. If now you will spare us, we will make amends to you and repay all that we have had at your expense. We will, each one of us, bring you oxen, gold, silver and bronze. Until then you are right to be angry and threaten us. Do but be merciful, and we will be loyal to you and rejoice at your homecoming."

"Eurymachus," said Odysseus sternly, "I shall never forgive you, even though you were to hand over to me all your possessions and all your inheritance. To you and the other princes I say this: you must stay and fight in fair combat or you must turn and fly. You have no choice. But fly as you may, there are some among you who shall not escape death this day."

Panic seized the suitors, and Eurymachus spoke.

"Friends," cried he, "now you see that this man will not be calmed. Prepare yourselves to fight. Draw your sharp swords. Make for yourselves a screen by turning the tables on their sides, so that they will protect you from his arrows."

With these words he drew his two-edged bronze sword from its sheath, uttered a terrible cry and leaped upon Odysseus. But at the same moment Odysseus let fly an arrow and struck Eurymachus in the breast. The suitor dropped his sword and fell to his knees. Then in his agony he smote the floor with his forehead, and the mists of death blinded his sight.

Next the hardy Amphinomus drew his sword and attacked Odysseus, but Telemachus flung his spear from behind and pierced Amphinomus between the shoulder-blades. This man too fell with a crash to the floor and died. Leaving his spear in the body of his victim, Telemachus ran to his father's side and said:

"Father, if we are to fight, it will be better if we are armed. Let me go to the armoury and bring you a helmet, a shield and two spears. I will do the same for myself, for Eumaeus and for Philoetius."

"Run and bring them." answered Odysseus, "while I still have arrows to fight off the enemy, who will try to drive me from the threshold."

So Telemachus ran to the armoury and brought out eight spears, four helmets and four shields. With these he clad himself and the two servants. Odysseus meanwhile killed as many of the suitors as he could with his arrows. When he had no more arrows, he leaned his bow against one of the door-posts and hung his shield about his shoulders. He donned the helmet that Telemachus had brought and grasped in either hand a bronze-tipped spear.

Now the only means of escape from the hall was a small postern door near to the threshold, and Odysseus told Eumaeus to guard this in case any tried to leave the hall. Meanwhile one of the suitors suggested that someone should escape by the postern and raise the hue and cry among their friends in the city so that help should come against Odysseus and his companions.

But Melanthius, the goat-herd said:

"That will not do, for it is hard to get out by the postern, which is so narrow that a single man might defend it. Let me go to the armoury unnoticed and bring you all arms and armour."

With this, Melanthius crept out of the hall unnoticed and went to the armoury. He came back carrying as many spears, helmets and shields as he could. He gave these to the suitors.

As soon as he saw that some of the suitors were armed, Odysseus felt fear in his heart, and he told Telemachus that either Melanthius, the treacherous goat-herd or one of the women had betrayed him.

"It is my fault," said Telemachus, "for in my haste I left the door of the armoury open, and one among the suitors has taken advantage of my mistake. Go at once, Eumaeus, and make fast the door of the armoury, and find out if you can whether, as I suspect, it is Melanthius who has taken the spears and the armour."

Melanthius went a second time to the armoury, and this time Eumaeus saw him.

"Odysseus," he said, "shall I go and kill that traitor Melanthius or bring him here for you to deal with?"

"You and the cow-herd", answered Odysseus, "shall go and seize Melanthius. Tie up his arms and legs and leave him in the armoury. Telemachus and I will stay here and see that none of the wooers leaves this hall."

M

At once Eumaeus and Philotius ran to the door of the armoury, and as Melanthius came out, carrying as many arms as he could, they seized hold of him and dragged him back into the armoury by the hair. Then they tied up his limbs with ropes and fastened another rope round his body. They threw the end over one of the roof-beams and hauled the wretched man up until he hung just below the roof.

"Hang there all night, miserable traitor," said Eumaeus, "until dawn, when it was your custom to drive goats here for the feasts of my master's enemies. Hang there all night, wretch."

With this Eumaeus closed the door of the armoury and returned with his companion to Odysseus' side.

So there they stood in the threshold, four brave men facing many desperate enemies. Then it was that Athene appeared at Odysseus' side in the likeness of his old friend Mentor.

"Mentor," Odysseus said, knowing he spoke to the goddess, "now come to our aid and keep us from harm."

She turned to Odysseus and spoke to him sternly:

"Odysseus," said the goddess, "why are you so faint-hearted? Did you not fight valiantly against the Trojans for nine long years, and have you lost heart now that you have come to your own house? Be of good heart, I say, and face these treacherous lords with fortitude."

Thus did the goddess encourage the man she had protected for so long. Then she flew up to the beams of the hall in the likeness of a swallow, perching there to watch what should befall.

Many of the wooers had by now been killed, but among the bravest of those who were left one of them spoke up and encouraged his companions saying:

"Come, friends, let us prepare to destroy Odysseus

and his son, for they have no help now that Mentor has left them. Do not aim all your spears at once, but let the six foremost among us attack the enemy."

At once six spears were flung at Odysseus and his friends but all failed, so powerful was Athene to help the man she protected. One spear struck the doorpost and another the door. Another stuck fast in the wall beside the threshold. Then Odysseus and his men threw their spears and, with the help of the goddess, four of the wooers were slain. At this the rest of the wooers drew back cowering in fear, and Odysseus and his men rushed forward and drew their spears out of the bodies. Then the wooers, inspired by the words of one of their leaders, once again attacked. This time Telemachus was struck on the wrist by a spear, and Eumaeus was grazed on the shoulder. Enraged by this attack, Odysseus and his men once more flung spears at the enemy, and each succeeded in killing one of the suitors. So the battle raged, and the hall was full of the groans of wounded men and the clash of arms upon armour. The floor ran with blood. The walls and the tables and stools were splashed with scarlet. Panic seized the wooers when they knew that the battle was going against them. One of them, the soothsayer, threw himself at Odysseus' feet and clasped him about the knees, begging for mercy.

"I did no evil in your hall, great Odysseus," he whined, "but tried always to hold back the others. I am only the soothsayer, who foretold their doom and strove to do good."

"If you are soothsayer to these wretches," answered Odysseus in his rage, "then you must often have told them I would never return. There is no mercy for you, coward and traitor that you are."

So saying, he seized a great sword and thrust it through the soothsayer's neck. While yet he whined for mercy, his body fell lifeless to the floor.

Then Phemius the minstrel sought in his turn to escape death. He had in his hand a lyre, and as he stood by the door, he wondered whether he should try to run away or whether he should appeal to great Odysseus. He decided that this was the better course. Flinging aside his instrument, he knelt before Odysseus and said:

"I beg you, mighty conqueror, to have mercy on me and spare my life. I came here, not as a wooer, but only to sing at the feasts of these men, who forced me to do their bidding. It will shame you in after time if you take the life of a minstrel, whose business it is to make music in the ears of gods and men. I shall sing before you as if you were a god, so do not be eager to cut off my head. Your own son Telemachus will bear me out in all I have said."

Telemachus stepped forward and said to his father:

"Do not kill this man. All he has said is true. He did not sing at his own will but was forced by the suitors, whom he had no power to resist. Spare this man, I beg you. And let us also spare Medon, the herald, who took care of me when I was a child and you were battling on the windy plains of Troy."

Now Medon was hiding under a table, covered with an oxhide. On hearing his name, he sprang out and clasped the knees of Telemachus. He thanked the young man for his words, and Odysseus smiled at him and said:

"My son has saved your life, Medon. You shall go forth and tell how your life was spared by the merciful Odysseus. Go and sit in a corner of the courtyard, away from the slaughter. Take Phemius the minstrel with you, for I will not harm either of you."

Then, while the two men went out into the court-yard, glad that their lives had been spared, but still fearful of what might befall them, Odysseus went about the hall to see if any of the suitors were yet living. Everywhere they lay in pools of blood, their bodies heaped upon one another like fish that the fishermen have drawn up in their nets and spilled upon the deck of their ship. He called his son to his side and told him to go to the women's rooms and fetch the old nurse Eurycleia.

When Eurycleia came into the hall and saw the bodies of the slain, a great joy filled her heart and she was going to cry out in triumph when Odysseus checked her and said:

"Rejoice in your heart, but do not express your joy aloud. It is not seemly to exult over the slain. These men have lost their lives because of their own wicked deeds and because they dishonoured the gods. The gods have avenged themselves upon those who dishonoured them. Let the women servants come into the hall and help my son and my two faithful companions to carry out the dead. Then let them wash the walls and the tables and the floor, so that my house may be cleansed of blood."

All was done as Odysseus commanded, and Melanthius, the false goat-herd, was put to death. Then a fire was lit and sulphur burnt in the hall to purify it from the taint of battle.

So the great slaughter was ended by which Odysseus regained his home and rid himself of its enemies. At last he told Eurycleia to bring forth her mistress Penelope.

18

Odysseus and Penelope

THE OLD NURSE Eurycleia hurried upstairs to her mistress' room. She chuckled to herself with delight as she went. Penelope was asleep on the bed, a smile of contentment on her features. Eurycleia shook her by the shoulder and Penelope opened her eyes.

"Wake up, madam, wake up!" cried the nurse. "What you have long dreamed of has come to pass. Come down and see for yourself. Odysseus has returned and has killed off the suitors. You will never more be troubled by them."

"Dear nurse," said Penelope with kindly disbelief, "has some god visited you and infected your brain? How could you wake me with such a fairy tale? I was enjoying the sweetest, the calmest sleep I have ever had since Odysseus sailed for Troy. If it had been one of the young girls who had told me such a story, I would have been angry. But I can't be angry with you."

"Dearest child," Eurycleia continued, taking little notice of Penelope's disbelief, "it is no fairy tale. Odysseus is in the house. He was that stranger, that beggar in disguise, whom everyone made sport of in the hall. Your son Telemachus knew who the stranger was, but he kept it a secret in obedience to his father.

Penelope jumped off the bed and threw her arms round the old woman's neck.

"Tell me one thing," she said. "If Odysseus has really returned, how could he fight the suitors alone—one man against so many?"

"I don't know," answered Eurycleia. "I did not see it, but I heard the groans of wounded and dying men. I and the other servants were shut in the inner room, until Telemachus sent for us. There stood Odysseus among the dead bodies. Now he is having the hall purified with burning sulphur. He has sent me to bring you to him, so that you may both rejoice together."

"This cannot be true," Penelope said. "It is not Odysseus, but some god. I shall never again see my husband."

It was indeed impossible for Penelope to believe in her husband's return. Since he had departed, twenty years had passed, and she had been wearied by false rumours and reports of his exploits and of his intention to return immediately. These reports had killed all hope in her breast.

Eurycleia sighed heavily and said:

"Will nothing make you believe? Here is another proof. When that stranger first arrived at our house, you may remember that it was I who washed his feet. I saw the very scar on his leg left by the wound he had from a wild boar when he was young. I longed to tell you, but Odysseus would not let me. Come now and see for yourself. If I am lying, you may take my life."

As the two women went to the hall, Penelope asked herself what she would do if the nurse's words were true. In the hall she sat on a stool by the fire in front of Odysseus. He stood by a pillar watching her. He waited for her to speak, but she said nothing. She was too distracted, and the words would not come. Penelope looked into Odysseus' face, longing to believe the nurse's words. But how could such a hero as her husband be dressed in those rags, and look so old and worn?

At last Telemachus broke the silence.

"Mother," he protested, "how can you be so unkind. Go to my father and embrace him. What other wife in the whole world would torture her husband in this way after his long years of suffering and hardship?"

"My son," said Penelope in a low voice, "I am lost in amazement and can find no words. I too have suffered for twenty years. Remember that. But if this is indeed my husband, he and I have secrets which no one else knows."

"Leave her, Telemachus," said Odysseus, smiling gravely. "Later she will test me. She cannot yet believe me to be her long lost husband because of my hideous rags."

He next took his son aside and told him that the men of Ithaca would come to revenge themselves for the death of their kinsmen, the suitors, and that he and his friends must be ready to fight. Meanwhile there must be dancing and singing in the house, so as to deceive any who came that way into thinking that nothing unusual had happened. So Telemachus gave orders that the household should assemble and minstrels play and sing. Before long the whole house rang with the sound of revelry. There was real joy in the hall, for all were delighted at the destruction of the enemies of Odysseus. And those who passed by outside said to one another:

"So at last the Queen has taken a husband from

among the suitors. She could wait no longer for her husband's homecoming. Hark how merrily they dance and make music."

While this was going on, Odysseus went and bathed himself and put on new and shining clothes, and Athene his protectress made him even more handsome than of old, and his hair fell in profusion about his strong shoulders. He went back to the hall and sat beside Penelope.

"Dear wife," he said, "how strange you are. What other woman would sit apart from her lord after so many years of separation? I never knew you had so hard a heart. Nurse," he continued, turning to Eurycleia, "make me a bed by myself, for this is the hardest-hearted woman alive."

At last Penelope spoke to Odysseus.

"Sir," she said, "you think me heartless, but I am not. Nor am I proud or disturbed in mind. But I cannot forget what you were like when your ship sailed for Troy. Go, then, nurse, do as he bids you. Bring out the bedstead from the marriage chamber that my husband built, and spread it here with blankets, so that he may sleep alone, as he commands."

These words were spoken to test Odysseus. He could bear it no longer, but burst out:

"Oh my wife, you stick a dagger in my heart. How can any man or woman bring my bedstead here? Do you not remember the great olive tree that grew in the court? It had a trunk as long and straight as a column of wood. I built my marriage chamber around it—I smoothed and shaped the trunk of that tree and made it into a bedpost. It became part of the bed. Is it still standing, or has someone cut down the tree and put up the bed somewhere else?"

Penelope ran to her husband weeping. How could she doubt him any longer? He alone could have known how his marriage bed had been constructed. She cried:

"O my husband, do not be angry with me because I did not at first know you. We have been kept apart all these years by the will of the gods. They alone have given us so much sorrow and suffering. I have always been afraid that some other man would come and deceive me, so I became suspicious. But now I know you for my true and only husband. Forgive me for not knowing you at once."

Odysseus, too, wept for joy and held her in his arms. She clung to him as a tired swimmer clings to a rock after escaping from a deadly storm and shipwreck.

"My dearest wife," Odysseus said, "there are yet more tasks to accomplish before we can enjoy peace in Ithaca, so let us now take our rest. I am weary after this day's terrible work."

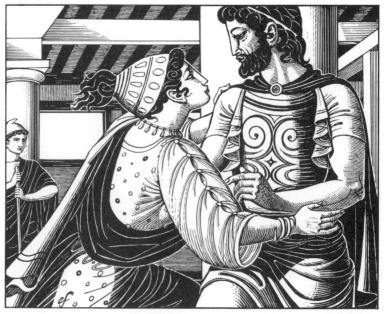

Penelope sent her servants to make ready their bed, and while this was being done, Odysseus and Penelope sat by the fire and talked together. He told her the story of many of his adventures, but they were too numerous to be related all in one evening. When the bed was ready, husband and wife went to their rest for the night, and the sound of music and dancing was silenced in the house of Odysseus.

Next morning Odysseus' first thought was for his old father, Laertes. He determined to go at once and greet him. He told his wife to remain indoors and speak to no one. Then he armed himself and ordered Telemachus, Eumaeus and Philotius, the cow-herd to do likewise. Together they went through the town, where no one saw them, and out into the country. Here Laertes stayed on his farm. He lived alone except for his labourers and an old serving woman who attended to him in the house. Odysseus told his three followers to go indoors and get ready a feast. He himself went into the fields to find Laertes. Odysseus found Laertes forking the earth round his fruit trees. The old man was wearing ancient leather garments, torn and mended. As Odysseus stood under a tree looking at the old man, bowed down with care and toil, the tears rolled slowly down his cheeks. He longed to rush up to his father and embrace him, but he thought it wise to speak to him first and find out what he was thinking. Odysseus went to where Laertes was digging, and as he spoke the old man straightened his back, leaned on his fork and looked into the eyes of the speaker. Odysseus said:

"You know how to care for an orchard, I see. You have figs and olives, vines and pears. How well you have tended them all. But if I may say so, it seems to me as if no one looks after you. You are old, and you can have given your master no cause why he should neglect you. But it looks to me as if you are too tall, too noble to be a slave to any man. You seem to me more like a king—one who should sleep softly at night and be honoured by your people. Who are you, and who is your master? I have but newly come here and am told I am in Ithaca. Is it really so? Once I received a stranger, who said his home was in Ithaca and his father was named Laertes. I took a liking to this guest, so that when he left me, I gave him rich presents— vessels of gold and silver and finely woven garments."

"Yes, my friend," the old man answered, "you are indeed in Ithaca, but things are not as they were. Thieves have come to rob us, and there is no one here to greet you as your friend would have greeted you if he had been alive still. But tell me, stranger, how long is it since you saw that man? He was my son, but he must have died long ago, far from his father and mother and his loving wife."

"It must be five years since we parted," replied Odysseus, with a sigh. "We had hoped to meet once more as host and guest."

At these words Laertes burst out weeping. He took dust from the earth and dropped it upon his grey hair in sign of mourning. When Odysseus saw this, he could not keep back his own tears, but threw his arms about his father and kissed him.

"Father," he said between his sobs, "grieve no longer. I am your own son Odysseus. I have come back at last and have slain the false princes in my own hall."

"If you are my son," Laertes said, stepping back and gazing hard at Odysseus, "give me some proof."

"Here is the scar made by the wild boar," Odysseus said, drawing back his cloak. "I can show you, too, every tree you planted for me in this orchard. When I was a boy, I followed you round and begged to be told the names of all the young trees. Some you gave me for my own—ten apples, thirteen pears and forty figs. You promised me fifty rows of vines that would be heavy with grapes when the gods sent rain and sun to make them grow."

Then Laertes knew that he was indeed talking to his own son. He would have fainted for joy had not Odysseus caught him in his arms and held him up. Soon, however, his strength returned and he gave thanks to Zeus for sending Odysseus back to Ithaca.

"Yet I am afraid, my son," he said. "I am afraid that if you have indeed killed the suitors, their kinsfolk and friends will get help and will revenge themselves upon you and all your house."

"Fear not," Odysseus said. "Let us go in and greet my son Telemachus. I sent him into your house to make ready a feast."

They went into the house, and while Odysseus looked round at the place he had not set foot in for twenty years, Laertes bathed himself and put on splendid clothes. When he came into the hall, he seemed to have grown taller and to have regained something of his youth and former strength. Odysseus told him that he looked as if some god had touched him, and Laertes answered:

"Oh, that the gods had given me strength and youth, that I might have fought at your side yesterday when you battled with the princes."

While they talked, the old servant went out and called in the labourers. As they reached the hall, Odysseus spoke to the eldest of them. This man had once been his own servant.

"Come in, my friends," Odysseus said. "It is a long time since I saw you last."

The old labourer hurried up to Odysseus, grasped his hand and pressed it to his lips. He gave thanks to the gods that his master had come back at last.

By this time the news of the battle had spread through the city. The friends and kinsmen of those who had been killed streamed to the hall of Odysseus and took away the bodies to be buried. Anger swelled in their hearts, and they cried out for vengeance. Foremost among the mourners was Eupeithes, father of Antinous, whom Odysseus had slain with an arrow as he was raising the wine cup to his mouth. He spoke to the people in the market-place.

"Listen to me," he cried, "while I tell you of the deeds of your king, Odysseus. Twenty years ago he took the bravest men of Ithaca and left them to perish at Troy or on the stormy seas. Now he has returned and butchered the finest of our sons. Are we not to be revenged on him? For my part I would rather share the death my son has died. Let us kill the tyrant!"

Some of the crowd showed pity for the anguish of Eupeithes, but others murmured among themselves and said the suitors had got no more than they deserved. Others told how the gods themselves had been on Odysseus' side. How else could so few have prevailed against so many? But Eupeithes gathered some of the people to his side and led them to the house of Laertes, where Odysseus was said to be.

But on Mount Olympus, home of the immortal gods, Athene spoke to her father Zeus.

"Will you say what you have decided," she asked.

"Is there now to be war or peace in far off Ithaca?"

Zeus, father of the gods, smiled and answered:

"It is you, my daughter, who has guided Odysseus through all his trials. Let it be you who decides his fate. As for me, I should be well pleased if an agreement were made between this man and his enemies, so that there might be peace and prosperity in rocky Ithaca."

Meanwhile the banquet was in progress in the house of Laertes, Odysseus told one of the servants to go out and see if his enemies were in sight. The servant returned at once and cried:

"They are coming. To arms, all of you!"

At once every man grasped what weapons he could lay hands on. Even Laertes, old as he was, strapped on his armour with trembling hands and followed his son out into the courtyard.

"Telemachus, my son," said Odysseus, who was at the head of the men, "be of good courage and fight like a hero, remembering the honour of our house."

"Father," answered Telemachus, "I will be a credit to you and our house."

"It is a proud day in my life," said Laertes, "when my son and my grandson swear loyalty to one another."

With that he flung his spear at Eupeithes, who fell, pierced through his helmet. Immediately Odysseus and Telemachus leapt towards the other intruders, brandishing their swords. But Athene, who had flown down from Olympus, raised her voice above the clash of weapons and cried:

"Fight no longer, men of Ithaca. Back—get back, I say!"

At the sound of the goddess's voice the followers of

Eupeithes trembled and turned pale. Their spears and shields dropped from their hands, and they ran in panic from the house of Laertes. Odysseus gave his battle-cry and ran after them, but Athene touched him on the shoulder and said:

"Odysseus, son of Laertes, sheath your sword and shed no blood. Otherwise you will anger my father Zeus, who sees all that men do on earth."

Odysseus instantly obeyed the goddess. In truth he was glad to do so, for he was wearied of fighting. Afterwards the goddess made an agreement between Odysseus and the friends and kinsmen of the dead suitors, so that they lived in peace together and the country prospered and was contented.